"This book gives language to the emerging forms of evangelism we see surfacing in many places—from a revised understanding of our role as Christ's ambassadors to the roles of friendship, community, narrative and invitation in helping people discover new life. Readers will experience *Reimagining Evangelism* as a breath of 'cosmic fresh air'!"

GEORGE G. HUNTER, DISTINGUISHED PROFESSOR OF EVANGELIZATION, SCHOOL OF WORLD MISSION AND EVANGELISM, ASBURY THEOLOGICAL SEMINARY

"Rick Richardson loves evangelism but hates clichés. Many believers (and unbelievers) have come to think of those two words as being inextricably linked. But Richardson is not about to surrender the spiritual practice of soul care for the people Jesus misses most to a religious marketing machine gone bad. In *Reimagining Evangelism* he introduces us to postmodern cultural realities and challenges us to see the big story of Jesus. A must read for people who are done with programs but need a new paradigm to help them navigate the cultural twists and turns they find themselves swimming in."

JIM HENDERSON, FRONTMAN FOR *OFF THE MAP*, AND AUTHOR OF *A.K.A. "LOST"*

"I love Rick Richardson's view of evangelism as a journey with people who are moving toward God. It breaks the old perspective of evangelism as only getting people to cross the conversion line. How freeing! And imagine when that idea is coupled with the reality that it takes a community to save a soul. Lights will go on for many with this important book."

LON ALLISON, DIRECTOR, BILLY GRAHAM CENTER, WHEATON COLLEGE

San Diego Christian College
2100 Greenfield Drive
El Cajon, CA 92019

"This book is fresh, provocative and insightful. If you've been running from the 'E-word,' let Richardson give you a new vision for what evangelism can look like in your life, and in this culture. You'll be surprised—and motivated! Rick is a source of teaching you can trust; grounded in orthodoxy but proven in experience."

MARK MITTELBERG, INTERNATIONAL WRITER AND SPEAKER, AND COAUTHOR OF *BECOMING A CONTAGIOUS CHRISTIAN*

"I loved this book. It's so warm, inviting and full of stories I can relate to. *Reimagining Evangelism* teaches and models how to share your faith in a way you will like—and so will your friends."

KEVIN A. MILLER, VICE PRESIDENT, CHRISTIANITY TODAY INTERNATIONAL

"*Reimagining Evangelism* is a book that every Christ-follower should read! Rick Richardson takes a word (evangelism) that scares all of us and helps us see it as something adventuresome. *Reimagining Evangelism* is all about building spiritual friendships, living in community and going on a great excursion with God's Spirit. I love the challenge Rick gives us to help people find their way back to God."

DAVE FERGUSON, LEAD PASTOR, COMMUNITY CHRISTIAN CHURCH/ NEWTHING NETWORK

269.2
R524r

13.⁰⁰

REIMAGINING EVANGELISM

Inviting Friends on a Spiritual Journey

RICK RICHARDSON

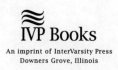

IVP Books
An imprint of InterVarsity Press
Downers Grove, Illinois

InterVarsity Press
P.O. Box 1400, Downers Grove, IL 60515-1426
World Wide Web: www.ivpress.com
E-mail: mail@ivpress.com

©2006 by Rick Richardson

All rights reserved. No part of this book may be reproduced in any form without written permission from InterVarsity Press.

InterVarsity Press® is the book-publishing division of InterVarsity Christian Fellowship/USA®, a student movement active on campus at hundreds of universities, colleges and schools of nursing in the United States of America, and a member movement of the International Fellowship of Evangelical Students. For information about local and regional activities, write Public Relations Dept., InterVarsity Christian Fellowship/USA, 6400 Schroeder Rd., P.O. Box 7895, Madison, WI 53707-7895, or visit the IVCF website at <www.intervarsity.org>.

All Scripture quotations, unless otherwise indicated, are taken from the Holy Bible, New International Version®. NIV®. Copyright ©1973, 1978, 1984 by International Bible Society. Used by permission of Zondervan Publishing House. All rights reserved.

Images: Royalty Free/Corbis

ISBN-10: 0-8308-3342-0

ISBN-13: 978-0-8308-3342-9

Printed in the United States of America ∞

Library of Congress Cataloging-in-Publication Data

Richardson, Rick, 1955-
  Reimagining evangelism: inviting friends on a spiritual journey /
  Rick Richardson.
    p. cm.
  Includes bibliographical references.
  ISBN-13: 978-0-8308-3342-9 (pbk.: alk paper)
  ISBN-10: 0-8308-3342-0 (pbk.: alk. paper)
  1. Witness bearing (Christianity) 2. Evangelistic work. I. Title.
  BV4520.R5195 2006
  269'.2—dc22

                                                                        2006013023

| P | 21 | 20 | 19 | 18 | 17 | 16 | 15 | 14 | 13 | 12 | 11 | 10 | 9 | 8 | 7 | 6 | 5 | 4 | 3 |
| Y | 24 | 23 | 22 | 21 | 20 | 19 | 18 | 17 | 16 | 15 | 14 | 13 | 12 | 11 | 10 | 09 | 08 |

CONTENTS

FOREWORD

I wondered how it would affect me—leaving pastoral ministry after twenty-four years, I mean, would I still be a faithful, energetic, faith-sharing Christian when I wasn't being paid to do so? How much of my zeal was related to my profession?

I remembered back to the days before I began working for the church, back when I was a college English instructor, an educational consultant, a grad student, a college student, a high school student. I had become a committed Christian in my teenage years, and without ever being pressured or trained to "evangelize," I developed a love for getting into conversations with people about God.

Yes, I loved Bible studies and worship gatherings, but even more, I loved to hang out with friends who weren't Christians. I loved answering their questions, asking them questions, talking naturally about matters of faith and commitment. I loved inviting them to the fellowship group I was part of. I loved helping them discover what it means to be a follower of Christ and then helping them grow in that new way of life.

Through the years, that love flowered. I was part of two church-planting endeavors before I was thirty. The second one began when my wife and I invited some friends from the university over to our home on Thursday nights—for homemade soup and fresh bread and conversation about God. That group grew and gradually morphed into a church that eventually became my life's work . . . for twenty-four years.

After my last Sunday as senior pastor, after an emotional send-off from the congregation that meant (and still means) so much to us, I felt a certain sense of sadness, to be sure, but also a sense of curiosity. What would it be like to be a "normal Christian" again—someone who doesn't always have a sermon to prepare? Someone who introduces himself not as a pastor but as an author?

A few days later, I was waiting for a plane about midnight in some city in the Midwest—I can't even remember where. There had been engine problems during a layover, and we had been sitting in a sterile departure gate area for a long time, waiting for news of when we would finally get home. A young man caught my eye a few places down in the row of fixed, uncomfortable seats. "Do you know if they have ATMs in the Baltimore airport?" he asked.

"Yes, there's one between Concourse B and C," I said. Then I felt something, a certain awareness or sense that's hard to describe if you've never experienced it. "Do you need money for something?" I asked.

"I need to catch a cab when I get to Baltimore," he said. Without really thinking about what I was offering, more just responding to this hard-to-explain inner urge, I said, "I'll give you a ride. Where are you going?" Common sense would have had me ask the question before making the offer, but that's how it happened.

Then the conversation flowed. He was on leave from the army, stationed in Germany, afraid that he was going to be sent to Iraq soon. He was just nineteen, going to see his mom. Somehow, we started talking about religion, God, faith, Christianity. He told me about the hypocrites he knew. He told me why he didn't follow any religion. The more I listened—without judgment, without trying to correct or "fix" him—the more he became open to and interested in what I had to say about my own faith, the reason for the hope that I have.

I think he learned some things through our conversation. I know I did—among them, that I still loved talking to people about God even when I wasn't being paid to. That people really need conversation partners on the spiritual journey. That books like the one you're holding are really important because you never know what's happening inside the soul of a person sitting next to you.

I'm thankful for Rick Richardson, and this book. If you read it— alone or, even better, with a group—you'll find yourself more ready, and more motivated, to be there for people like my new nineteen-year-old friend. I gave him my e-mail address. I hope he'll stay in touch.

I hope you'll take this book to heart and put it to practice in your life.

Brian McLaren

FOREWORD

Throughout history, evangelism has constantly been readapted to cultures, languages and the tides of politics. Not the message however—only the delivery systems. The apostle Paul, fully anointed by the Holy Spirit, spelled it out most pointedly: "I have become all things to all men so that by all possible means I might save some" (1 Corinthians 9:22).

But as Rick Richardson so clearly points out, once again, times are changing, paradigms are shifting, and the world of evangelism needs to be rethought, reshaped and reimagined. It's time for us all to step up and take our own important roles in daily evangelism. This one fact alone has helped me to understand—very forcefully—how I can better know this generation. I've learned a lot, and discuss it with my wife on a regular basis. I want to better present our Lord Jesus Christ.

For the past forty years I've traveled the world sharing the true story of Jesus Christ. It's a great story—the greatest ever told, a story of eternal consequences, promises of hope, freedom and all that is joyful. But sadly, it's a message that isn't heard that often in the world today.

Deep down, everyone is interested in this message of hope, whether they want to admit it or not. And more and more, I'm surprised to run into people who clearly have no idea who Jesus Christ is and what he has done for them.

Just like you, I feel a burden to share this good news with those around me. And I'm happy to see a book like *Reimaging Evangelism: Inviting Friends on a Spiritual Journey* that helps us identify the issues and problems keeping us from sharing this good news on a regular basis with this generation. People think differently now, and perceive differently than the past. So you and I need to learn how to share the great news of Jesus Christ so it will be understood. Rick teaches me, and I hope you too, how to evangelize today, not in the 1900s.

It never ceases to amaze me that God allows *us* to take part in sharing his love—his good news gospel—with others. Yes, the Great Commission (Matthew 28:18-20) *commands* us to go and share. But more than that, it's a blessing. Who would thoughtfully choose anything else?

I can't tell you how many stories I hear of friends who have been completely changed by the simple experience of sharing their faith with someone else. It's an exciting thing, and it's not that hard. It simply requires us to be open and honest and aware of God's leading.

The hardships we face, the joys we encounter, even the struggles we deal with on a daily basis—they all have extreme power in sharing our faith with others.

To tell you the truth, my message hasn't changed at all over the years. God gave me one message—Jesus Christ—and I will share him faithfully. Just like Corrie ten Boom, a Holocaust survivor, once said, "For all these years, I've been going all over the world with one message: There is no pit so deep that the love of God is not deeper still."

Corrie ten Boom shared her story. Nothing more. And through it, she reached thousands, possibly millions, with the good news of Jesus Christ. Are you prepared to do the same?

Studying Rick's book prayerfully, you will also learn to share the Savior of the world winsomely. Few things in this life compare.

Thanks, Rick, for making us think creatively, honestly and powerfully.

Luis Palau

ACKNOWLEDGMENTS

I am deeply grateful to the many friends who have invested in this book. Special thanks go to the National Evangelism Champions Team with InterVarsity, and to my colleagues Lon Allison, Jerry Root, John Armstrong, Scott Moreau, Evvy Campbell and Carol Fowler who help make the masters in evangelism program at Wheaton such a delight to lead. In addition, Doug Schaupp, Sandra Van Opstal, Brenda Salter McNeil, Peter Cha, Peter Hong and Daniel Hill made specific comments to increase the book's impact in multiethnic student and local church contexts.

I also profoundly appreciate the generosity and spirit of encouragement John Jones gave to this project. His convictions about the power of the gospel and the truth of the faith were challenging and important.

As always, my gratitude to my beloved family, Chris, Steve, Colby and MaryKay, cannot be expressed in words.

This book is dedicated to my many dear friends, colleagues and partners in the gospel in InterVarsity Christian Fellowship and InterVarsity Press these last twenty-five years.

I am especially grateful to Terry Erickson, my evangelism partner with InterVarsity, and to Andy Le Peau and Ruth Goring, my editors with InterVarsity Press.

1

REIMAGINING EVANGELISM

Salespeople or Travel Guides?

Over the years, evangelism has gotten a bad name. It is sales, manipulation, TV preachers, big hair, pushing people to convert and going door to door. It elicits feelings similar to the intrusive practice of telemarketing. As Becky Pippert quips in her book *Out of the Saltshaker,* it is something you wouldn't want to do to your dog, much less a person you like.

Evangelism has always had image problems. But the image problems for evangelism have only gotten worse in recent years. Photos of religious people, true believers, running planes into buildings and suicide bombing innocent men, women and children have only reinforced the pervasive conviction in our society that people who think they know the truth and that everybody else is wrong are not only misguided but positively dangerous.

How did we get to this place? How did a word that means "good news" get such bad press? And is there a way beyond the present impasse? Can we redeem the word—and the practice of evangelism?

The time has come to examine, and perhaps jettison, our old paradigms and pictures of evangelism. The time has come to reimagine how we picture and practice sharing the good news about Jesus.

The time has come because the old pictures and practices aren't wearing well and aren't working well. People in our culture aren't responding. And people in the church aren't excited or engaged.

Many believers are as uncomfortable with and turned off by evangelism as the irreligious are.

The time has come because our culture is shifting. We are moving from a modern, rationalistic, technique-oriented culture to a more imaginative, experiential and story-oriented culture. Our memorized scripts and canned techniques may have helped an older generation reach out to the unchurched, but at this point in history, our techniques and scripts are more a hindrance than a help.

The time has come because God is at work in new ways. People today are spiritual but not dogmatic. They want to know that God is *real* and not merely reasonable. They are looking for stories and experiences and connection to God more than logic and proof and reasons for God. And in the midst of this growing hunger for authenticity and reality, God is moving and God's Spirit is manifesting in powerful new ways.

The time has come because the West is no longer leading the way. Our teachers and mentors in the evangelism adventure are now African and Asian and Latin American peoples. The balance of spiritual power in the world is shifting to the global South. People who have suffered persecution, served the poor in their midst and learned to love their enemies have an evangelistic vitality that is contagious. They are now calling us to recover our spiritual vigor. We in the West are now more learners and receivers than leaders and senders. And the most crucial thing we are relearning from our brothers and sisters in the global South is the role and reality of the Holy Spirit in witness.

These are very exciting days in the life of the church. The time has come; the gospel can be renewed in our day, for it is the power of God for salvation. Let us listen to what God is saying by the Holy

Spirit and commit ourselves to reimagining evangelism for our generation.

THE OLD IMAGE

What is the Spirit saying to the church today about evangelism? Is the Spirit of God leading us into new ways to picture and practice evangelism and witness?

Some people argue for getting rid of the word *evangelism* entirely. One friend of mine calls his whole approach to evangelism "Non-evangelism for the Rest of Us." I have great sympathy for his desire to overcome the barriers that the E-word brings up in many of us. But evangelism is biblical, and it is as crucial to the life of the church and the purposes of God as ever. We need new vision, new pictures and practices, not merely a rejection of the word *evangelism*.

But before we find our way to the new pictures and practices, we should review what the old pictures and practices were.

The paradigm that dominated much twentieth-century evangelism might be called "Evangelism as Closing the Deal on a Sales Call." Many Christians think they have to dump their content on someone and then close the deal, or else they haven't really shared their faith. This basic paradigm of evangelism as individuals seeking to make the close on a sales call permeates the evangelical consciousness. Our image of the evangelist is the image of a spiritual salesman.

This paradigm of evangelism is a barrier to Christians, for it leaves them feeling like they don't really have a part to play in it. If they aren't extroverted, persuasive, an expert on their product, skilled at responding to the questions that will come up, and able to be pushy and assertive when it comes to making the close, then they don't identify with evangelism as part of their life and gifts. People often say to me some version of the following: "I don't like to push things on people if they don't want them. I'm kind of introverted, I'm not good at arguing with people, I avoid conflict, and I hate awkwardness in relationships. So evangelism is not for me. I feel guilty that I don't share my faith. But I feel inadequate, shut down and even inauthentic about becoming an extroverted crusader for God."

Such sentiments are widespread and debilitating. We feel like a salesperson selling a product that people mostly don't want. We are shut down because we are going by a script that doesn't work for us, and we have pictures and practices that don't fit us or the people we want to reach out to.

But we *can* recover our confidence and excitement. If we believed that God is at work everywhere and we're more like a detective discovering clues and a guide sharing wisdom, then evangelism would feel very different. We can look for God to be at work always and everywhere.

Before I explore the new image of evangelism, let me anticipate two criticisms people may make about this chapter and this book. First, some will say I have set up a straw man: I have caricatured the old model and thus set up the new model for easy acceptance. I agree. I have set up a straw man. But I have done so for an important reason. Many people in the church *and* many people outside the church have exactly this model, this straw man, in their minds, and it is a major barrier to many Christians' embracing evangelism as part of their life.

Second, people will notice where I have focused. I am focused on people who don't feel especially gifted in evangelism. I am very supportive of people who feel called to proclaim the gospel publicly, but this book is not primarily addressed to them. The average person who wants to love and follow Jesus has much more to give their spiritual friends and potential spiritual friends than they are presently giving. It is that immense potential that I hope this book, and the Holy Spirit, will unlock and unleash.

If regular folks like us are filled with the Spirit and led by the Spirit and pursue conversations with spiritual companions, we may be used by God to change the face of the church and contribute much toward the redemption of people and the transformation of society. That's where I have chosen to focus.

So let's explore a new image of evangelism.

WITNESSES AS TRAVEL GUIDES

In the Scripture, the word *evangelism* means "communicating or announcing good news." Based on that, let's try seeing ourselves as travel guides on a spiritual journey rather than traveling salespeople on a call. To make this mental shift, we can picture Gandalf and Galadriel, Frodo and Samwise instead of TV preachers and door-to-door salesmen. Gandalf and Galadriel, Frodo and Samwise are all characters in J. R. R. Tolkien's *Lord of the Rings* books, which Peter Jackson turned into a blockbuster movie trilogy, the last of which won the Academy Award for best picture. I have loved Tolkien's fantasy for many years, and as I open myself to reimagine evangelism, these works of fantasy provide some wonderful pictures of how to pursue conversations with friends on a journey.

The hero of the books is Frodo Baggins, a hobbit. Hobbits are little people with hairy feet who love the simple pleasures of life: smoking pipeweed, drinking ale, gardening and dining many times a day. Frodo goes on a journey to destroy the great Ring of

Power—a symbol of the temptation to dominate and control others and our world. In that sense, Frodo's journey is above all a spiritual journey, and along the way he is accompanied by travel guides who function as good "evangelists." You might also call them spiritual mentors. Some you may be able to identify with, and some you may not. But all of them practice the art of spiritual guidance at key moments in Frodo's spiritual quest in ways that you may find applicable to your relationships with seekers and skeptics.

A WIZARD'S WISDOM

Gandalf is a wise person who not only gives good advice and guidance but above all exemplifies a well-lived life. One of his most striking "evangelism" moments with Frodo comes on a journey through caves and tunnels under a mountain. These tunnels, the Mines of Moria, were built by the race of the dwarves.

Gandalf is leading the company of travelers through the tunnels and comes to a three-way fork in the road. Unsure of which direction to take, Gandalf pauses, lights his pipe and considers the options. Frodo approaches Gandalf, because he has seen a creature following the company through the mines. This creature turns out to be Gollum. Gollum held the Ring of Power for many years and fell into spiritual ruin as a result of his addiction. He had possessed the Ring, and the Ring had come to possess him. He then had lost the Ring to Frodo's uncle, Bilbo Baggins, and now spends his life trying to recover it. In a short and simple conversation, Gandalf shows us the art of being a spiritual travel guide for the journey.

FRODO: it's a pity that Bilbo did not kill him [Gollum] when he had a chance.

GANDALF: Pity—it was pity that stayed Bilbo's hand. Many that live deserve death, and some that die deserve life. Can you give it to them, Frodo? Do not be too eager to deal out death and judgment. Even the very wise cannot see all ends. My heart tells me that Gollum has some part to play yet for good or ill before this is over. The pity of Bilbo may rule the fate of many.

FRODO: I wish the ring had never come to me. I wish none of this had happened.

GANDALF: So do all that live to see such times, but that is not for them to decide. All we have to decide is what to do with the time that is given to us. There are other forces at work in this world, Frodo, besides the will of evil. Bilbo was meant to find the ring, in which case you also were meant to have it, and that is an encouraging thought.

Gandalf speaks just a few words, yet throughout the rest of the journey, Frodo returns again and again to these words. Gandalf has seen clues of "God" at work in Frodo's life, and he points the clues out. His words aren't cliché or obvious or overstated. He suggests that just maybe something much bigger is at work in Frodo's life than Frodo realizes. And then he helps Frodo to focus on the important issue: What next step will he take? How will he respond to the clues that he has? What will he do with the power of choice?

Couldn't you do that with friends on their spiritual journey? Couldn't you look for clues of God at work? Couldn't you make suggestions? You might say, "I wonder if what you're going through is a God-thing. I wonder if your spiritual doubts and struggles and experiences are a clue to something bigger that is at work in your life. What do you think? If so, how will you respond?" It may not sound like much. But I believe identifying clues of the presence of the Spirit in the lives of seekers and skeptics is at the heart of the image of evangelism that God wants to challenge us with.

AN ELF QUEEN'S VULNERABILITY

During the journey through the darkness of Moria, the company endures a battle in which Gandalf apparently falls to his death. The others make it through and, in great grief and despair from the loss of Gandalf, arrive in the Elven land of Lothlorien, ruled by the elf queen Galadriel (played by Cate Blanchett in the movie).

While others sleep, Frodo and Galadriel meet late at night in a grove, and Galadriel shows Frodo the future if his quest should fail. Then they have a "spiritual guidance" conversation.

FRODO: If you ask it of me, I will give you the One Ring.

GALADRIEL: You offer it to me freely. I do not deny that my heart has greatly desired this. In place of a dark Lord you will have a Queen, not dark but beautiful and terrible as the dawn, treacherous as the sea, stronger than the foundations of the earth. All shall love me and despair.

She stood before Frodo seeming now tall beyond measurement, and beautiful beyond enduring, terrible and worshipful. Then she let her hand fall, and the light faded, and suddenly she laughed again, and lo! She was shrunken: a slender elf-woman, clad in simple white, whose gentle voice was soft and sad.

GALADRIEL: I pass the test. I will diminish, and go into the West, and remain Galadriel.

FRODO: I cannot do this alone.

GALADRIEL: You are a Ring Bearer, Frodo. To bear a ring of power is to be alone. This task was appointed to you, and if you do not find a way, no one will.

FRODO: Then I know what I must do. It's just—I'm afraid to do it.

GALADRIEL: Even the smallest person can change the course of the future.

Galadriel gives Frodo a great gift. She shows him her soul. She reveals the temptation with which she struggles. She becomes vulnerable about her own soul's darkness. But she also shares her triumph. She chooses the way of humility and sanity and wholeness. She will remain true to who she is, even if that means she will diminish or die.

Often we think of evangelism as sharing our strengths, having it all together spiritually. We think that's what it means to be a witness. Galadriel opens to our imagination a different way. Our weakness, our story of struggle, even the truth about the cost of our choice to follow God—these are the greatest gifts we have to give to others in their journey.

Good travel guides know that stories of failure and struggle and doubt, of wrong turns and missed opportunities, are as important and compelling for other travelers as stories of success. They are the "humanizing" dimension of the story of the journey and the source of many of the most important lessons and pointers along the way. They help us know that we are all on a similar journey and can fail in similar ways.

Did you ever think that the greatest gift you could give to your seeking and skeptical friends is the story of your spiritual struggles and doubts? As you reveal some of the vulnerability and even the darkness of your soul, along with your choice to be true to who you are despite the cost, your friends will listen. Your authority in part comes from your authenticity, the authenticity of your struggles and your flawed humanity.

EVANGELISM HOBBIT STYLE

The last "evangelistic" moment I want to raise from the Lord of the Rings movies comes out of an interaction between Frodo and his faithful friend and companion Samwise Gamgee, or Sam.

Sam has just saved Frodo from being carried away by an enemy and has pulled Frodo back from the brink of being swallowed up by his addiction to the Ring of Power. And Frodo resents it, is furious. The Ring has gained increasing power over Frodo's will. He is at a very dark moment in his spiritual journey, and he does something that is terrible. Drawing a knife on his most faithful friend, he comes close to stabbing him for his interference. If you have ever confronted a friend or family member who is being swallowed up by an addiction, you will have some idea of the scene.

Sam, this little hobbit, very simple and down to earth and not often good with words, shines very brightly at this moment in the art of spiritual guidance.

SAM: It's me. It's your Sam. Don't you know your Sam?

[Frodo puts the knife away and falls back.]

FRODO: I can't do this, Sam.

SAM: I know. It's all wrong. By rights, we shouldn't even be here. But we are. It's like in the great stories, Mr. Frodo, the ones that really matter. Full of darkness and danger they were. And sometimes you didn't want to know the end, because how could the end be happy? How could the world go back to the way it was because so much bad happened? But in the end, it's only a passing thing. This shadow, even darkness, must pass. A new day will come. And when the sun shines, it will shine out the clearer. Those were the stories that stayed with you, that meant something, even if you were too small to understand why. But I think, Mr. Frodo, I do understand. I know now. Folk in those stories had lots of chances of turning back, only they didn't. They kept going because they were holding on to something.

FRODO: What are we holding on to, Sam?

[Sam takes Frodo, helps him to his feet, looks into his eyes and speaks with quiet conviction.]

SAM: That there's some good in this world, Mr. Frodo, and it's worth fighting for.

Sam tells the Great Story, what we who are followers of Christ would call the "kingdom story." He gives Frodo hope. He points the way forward. He invites Frodo to understand his part in the story of the triumph of goodness over evil and life over death.

So often we package the gospel in ways that make it seem irrelevant to our daily lives and to the course of current events. But Sam has understood it is all a part of a larger story that has meaning and purpose and direction. And we can each be part of that bigger story.

Evangelism is telling the story of God's ultimate victory over the darkness, in our world and in our own soul. Evangelism is inviting people to take their part in that big story. Sam is not very articulate. Nor does he take himself too seriously. But he knows the story, and he sees the point of it. When Frodo is in need, when he is close to despair and ready to give up, Sam is ready to tell the story and remind Frodo that he has a place in it. He challenges Frodo not to give up and not to go back.

How can we become such storytellers? How can we recover the dimensions of the bigger story that will speak to the seeking friends with whom we are on the journey? How can we get beyond the packaged gospel to the good news of hope and healing and victory over the darkness?

Together, I hope these images begin to awaken in your heart a new hunger to reimagine evangelism and to take your part as a witness, a journey guide.

NEW WAYS TO CONNECT AND
COMMUNICATE THE GOOD NEWS

This image of the evangelist as travel guide and the definition of evangelism as conversations with people on a spiritual journey lead to shifts in our pictures and practices at every point. Here are the shifts in pictures and practices that we will explore in this book.

Collaboration versus activism. Most of us get tired just thinking about evangelism. Our old model directs us to share the good news with everybody all the time, whether we know them well or not and whether spiritual conversation is appropriate or not. We must build friendships, talk to strangers, study the Bible with unchurched people, share the gospel, call them to Christ and then follow up. Don't you just get tired reading that list, let alone thinking about doing it? And yet we feel like anything less falls short.

What if we rediscovered the role and reality of the Holy Spirit? What if we saw ourselves as collaborators rather than activists, looking for clues about where God is already at work, expecting God to nudge us, being in an attitude of prayer whenever we were with unchurched people? Evangelism could become an adventure in detection rather than a burden of making it all happen.

Community versus individual. God is far more committed to raising up witnessing *communities* than to raising up witnessing *individuals.* Our sales model leads us to think of individual salespeople fanning out across the landscape, going door to door and person to person. Though individual witness is certainly important, the Holy Spirit fills a Christian community and uses the community as a body in witness. Each member has its own particular contribution to make, according to the gifts each person has been given. More important than each of us doing the same thing to witness to others, we each must do our particular part. Then our witness together will be much greater than the sum of our parts.

Further, today people come to Christ primarily in the context of community. Belonging comes before believing. Evangelism is about helping people belong so that they can come to believe. So our communities need to be places where people can connect before they have to commit.

Friendship versus agenda. Our old model focuses on the agenda—downloading our content and closing our deal. We easily assume that if we haven't shared the whole ball of wax and challenged people to commit their lives, we haven't done evangelism. But the model of conversations with spiritual friends delights in the relationship itself and rejoices over every spiritual conversation. As Brian McLaren likes to say, we count conversations and not just conversions. So we learn the art of spiritual friendship and authentic conversation.

Story versus dogma. Our old picture focuses on certain truths or beliefs we are to communicate. The sin of humanity, the judgment of God and the sacrifice of Christ as he takes the just judgment of God on the cross in our place are some of the primary truths we are to communicate. If we haven't communicated those particular truths, we feel we haven't evangelized. The new model doesn't lose those truths but realizes we don't start there. People today are much more concerned about an experiential reality of God than about dogmas and beliefs. Whenever we have been able to tell a story about God's reality, then we have had good spiritual conversation. We have evangelized!

The outside-the-box Jesus versus the cliché Jesus. People in our culture think they know what Jesus is about. And many are intrigued by Jesus, but they don't want to talk about Jesus with church types. Church types seem to have Jesus in a box and talk about Jesus in very uninteresting ways. Our old model emphasizes bringing up Jesus and the benefits of Jesus whenever possible. And so the recipients of this sales approach never know when Jesus might pop up. It might be anytime, but they always know what he will look like. He's kind and good, saves you, fulfills you, and is the answer to any question you might have, and lots of questions you don't have.

The new model brings up Jesus naturally and in noncliché ways. Jesus surprises people not by popping out at every moment but by looking very different from what was expected when he does appear.

Good news about God's kingdom versus good news about the afterlife. The old model emphasized how we could be forgiven of our sins and go to heaven after we die. But actually that wasn't Jesus' focus, though it was part of his message. Jesus' main message was that the kingdom or rule of God is at hand. The rule of God is the act of God to set things right and to make people and the world work as they were intended to work. So Jesus talked much more about this life than about the next, much more about changing this world than about giving us a free pass to the next.

Journey versus event. Our model of conversion has pushed us to draw lines in order to figure out who's in and who's out, and we look for a one-time event, a decision, that distinguishes people on the outside from those on the inside. I don't know about you, but for me this constant attempt to figure out who has become a Christian and who's in and who's out has been a very frustrating and fruitless experience. The new model, a model based on the image of journey, sees all of us as moving either toward the goal or away from the goal. If the goal is to be a wholehearted follower of Jesus, then we are at different points along the way. But the crucial question is whether we are moving toward the center and beginning to follow in the footsteps of the Leader.

Each chapter will look at one of the shifts in our picture and practice of evangelism. We will explore the shift, see if Scripture backs it up, look honestly at barriers and brainstorms to help us pursue the new model, and end with some practical skills that can get us ready for the challenges that will face us on the spiritual friendship adventure.

Through each of these explorations, we will look to the Holy Spirit to teach us and lead us. After all, the Holy Spirit is the true witness to Jesus. The Holy Spirit has been pursuing conversations with people he loves on a spiritual journey for the past two millennia. The Holy Spirit has much to teach us if we will listen and learn.

A final word: Although the sales model is the box people of our culture have most commonly put evangelism in, the relational evangelism model can itself be a box. We can build trust and friendship with people but never get to the point of challenge. People are not loved when we build trust but never communicate truth. So the new model, the new ways of communicating and connecting, must transcend the relational evangelism box just as much as they transcend the sales box. We need a fresh wind of the Spirit, and new ways to connect and communicate, so that God can set his people free for transformational witness. Even the emphasis on friendship, though healthy and wise can hold us back. We can learn to look to the Holy Spirit, build trust, and share ourselves and our faith authentically with others, whether we have just met them or known them for years.

Reimagining evangelism can help set us free for authentic and Spirit-empowered witness. But risk is inescapable. If we are looking for risk-free evangelism, we will never influence people toward Christ.

So are you ready for the adventure of spiritual companionship, conversation and challenge? Are you ready to share what wisdom and experience you have with others? If so, let's go!

2

REDISCOVERING THE HOLY SPIRIT
Collaboration Versus Activism

I met Jan on the trolley in Amsterdam. I was making my daily trek to the Internet café to connect with friends and family back at home. As I looked at the passing canals, my eyes came to rest on Jan, standing near me. He was looking around and looking dejected. I felt a nudge from the Holy Spirit to talk to him.

I said something like "Such a beautiful city."

He asked if I was just visiting. I told him I was in Amsterdam for a conference sponsored by Billy Graham at the main hall in town.

He opened up quickly. He had been religious in the past, but not now. He had lived in Amsterdam for four years and had found it difficult. He asked me if I had ever been to the red-light district. I told him I had passed by it but not gone into it. He started to share that he had visited a few times. "Sometimes I get lonely and just need something." He then admitted that visiting the Red Light District had ruined his last serious relationship with a woman. She hadn't understood, and he hadn't gotten over the breakup. He was hurt and angry still. And the end result was that he was achingly lonely.

Our stop came. As we got off the trolley, I asked if I could pray for him. He welcomed my prayers. "Certainly can't hurt," he quipped.

So amid a light mist outside an Amsterdam trolley station, I stood next to Jan and prayed. I cried out to God for Jan's loneliness and pain. I prayed for God's blessing and healing in his life. I asked

God to minister to the lonely places that had led him to seek comfort with prostitutes, a quest that had resulted in even deeper loneliness. I prayed about his broken relationship with a woman and his pain, anger and even bitterness over it. I prayed for his peace and for him to find his way back home to God. I prayed for him to be strengthened and convicted to face the hard issues and wrong choices in his life and be reconciled to others.

At the end of the prayer time, Jan just stood there with a tear in his eye, saying he hadn't felt such a presence and peace for years. God was present, and this man knew it and responded. I could see that he could have stood there next to me and in the presence of God for as long as I was able to stay. When it was time to go, I left with deep joy filling my heart. I had gotten to collaborate with what the Holy Spirit was doing. I hadn't made it all happen. I had merely responded to God's work in another and God's work in me.

Was it a risk to ask Jan if I could pray for him? Yes. He could have said no, or we both could have felt very awkward. But the chance of him taking a step toward God was well worth the risk of me feeling rejected. Because it's not about me. It's about God.

God was already at work in Jan before I got there. God worked powerfully in Jan's heart while we stood and talked and prayed together. I don't know what has happened since, but I am convinced that God has continued to work in Jan's heart, wooing him and convicting him and pursuing him. I was just one link in the chain of God's forging. I only had to play the part that God had nudged and called and invited me to play. And God could have used the experience even if Jan had said no.

Nothing would transform our pictures and practices of evangelism like rediscovering the role of the Holy Spirit and learning to go along for the ride.

Discovering and collaborating with the Holy Spirit in witness would also revolutionize our sense of the authority we ourselves have as witnesses. God goes before us. God is there with us. God remains after us. God redeems and God intervenes. Our authority as witnesses emerges out of our union with Christ through the Holy Spirit. Whenever you speak of Christ with another, you do not stand alone. God is with you, in front and behind, before and after. We can rest in that authority and be secure in God's presence with us to convict, to heal and to save. Witness is not about us. It's about God, and God's presence in the journey of others.

Whenever I read the Scriptures and observe evangelism, the dominant thing I notice is the role of the Holy Spirit. The most explicitly evangelistic book of the Bible, the book of the Acts of the Apostles, would better be called the book of the Acts of the Holy Spirit. The Holy Spirit is the hero of the book of Acts and the primary witness to Jesus. The Holy Spirit heals, the Holy Spirit inspires people with the right words, the Holy Spirit gives boldness, the Holy Spirit opens doors; the Holy Spirit moves Philip out into the desert to talk to an Ethiopian and then back to Samaria to continue his work (see Acts 8). The Holy Spirit tells Peter not to call unclean what God has called clean and then sends him to a reach out to a Gentile soldier (see Acts 10). Then the Holy Spirit falls upon the Gentile soldier and his family to prove that he has accepted them. The Holy Spirit doesn't even wait to let Peter finish his little speech to the soldier and his family. The Holy Spirit acts *through* the apostles whenever he can, and *in spite of* the apostles whenever he has to. Peter preached a great first evangelistic sermon (see Acts 2), but no one would have listened if the Holy Spirit hadn't caused a ruckus first by speaking to all present in their own languages through uneducated people.

In the Gospel of John chapters 14 and 16, Jesus tells us that having the Holy Spirit is even better than having Jesus still in the flesh. The Holy Spirit convicts the world, leads us into all truth, speaks only what he has been told to speak and gives glory to the Son. The Spirit is always and everywhere the first and primary Witness. We are partners and collaborators with the Holy Spirit.

In other words, the first task of anyone who longs to reach out to others is learning to listen to God and collaborate with the Holy Spirit.

JESUS AND THE HOLY SPIRIT

Most people know Jesus did many miracles and knew a lot of things about people that he learned in some supernatural way. He healed lepers, blind people, lame people, paralyzed people, people with withered limbs and spiritually oppressed people. He knew Nathanael was a person of deep integrity when he had seen him only from afar (John 1:48). He knew the Samaritan woman had been married five times and was living with a man out of wedlock (John 4:17-18). He knew Lazarus wouldn't stay dead but would rise again (John 11:4). He knew Judas would betray him and Peter would deny him.

How did Jesus do all those miracles and know all those things? Some people think it was because he was God. Yes, Jesus was God, the only begotten Son. But I do not believe that Jesus did all those miracles and knew all those things because he was God. Jesus was fully human, and nothing Jesus did or said or knew violated his capacities as a finite human being. Scripture bears this out.

Paul tells us in Philippians 2:6-11 that Jesus did not hold on to his equality with the Father but emptied himself of all his divine prerogatives and transcendent powers and became a human being. He was genuinely human.

And then Luke tells us the secret of Jesus' power and knowledge:

> Jesus returned to Galilee in the power of the Spirit, and news about him spread through the whole countryside. (Luke 4:14)

The key is not that Jesus is divine, but that Jesus is filled with the Holy Spirit!

Jesus later tells his disciples they will do what he has been doing, and even greater things (John 14:12). How? When Jesus leaves, the Father will send the promised Holy Spirit.

In Acts, the disciples continue to do the works of Jesus and speak the words of Jesus. How? They have been filled with the Holy Spirit.

In John 5, Jesus speaks to a man, an invalid for thirty-eight years, who is lying by the side of a pool. Jesus asks him if he wants to be healed. The man doesn't even say yes. He just makes excuses for being unable to get into the pool when it is stirred up. People believed that the pool was stirred up by an angel, who would then heal the first person who got in.

Jesus cuts in on the man's excuses and tells him to get up, pick up his mat and start walking. To everyone's surprise, he gets up and walks. I can imagine that the most shocked person is the invalid himself! I can almost hear him as he looks down at his walking legs, saying to himself, *What are you doing, legs? What's up?*

The religious leaders, guardians of what is socially appropriate, are scandalized. Jesus has healed on the sabbath. I can hear them too. "You can't work on the sabbath, Jesus. It's not right. It's inappropriate. Let the man suffer by the side of the pool for another day.

Heal him tomorrow. Have some sense of propriety, for God's sake!"

Jesus has a very powerful answer for those religious types: "I tell you the truth, the Son can do nothing by himself; he can do only what he sees his Father doing, because whatever the Father does the Son also does" (John 5:19).

Here is Jesus' secret to powerful evangelism. He is a collaborator, a partner. He does only what he sees the Father doing.

Jesus is our model for witness, just as Jesus is our model for life. Our evangelism is often ineffective and guilt ridden because we think it all rides on us. Jesus reminds us that we can do nothing on our own. The only witness that bears fruit is collaborative witness, directed by the Holy Spirit.

Now God can lead us and use us in witness whether we are consciously collaborating with the Holy Spirit or not. But how much better if we begin to intentionally listen and discern what God is already doing so we can ride the wave of the Holy Spirit's witness in the lives of others. As Rick Warren reminds us in *The Purpose Driven Church*, "We should stop praying, 'Lord, bless what I'm doing' and start praying, 'Lord, help me to do what you are blessing.'"

Many people feel guilty that they don't witness more often. Learning to listen to the Holy Spirit could relieve a lot of guilt. We look to God to nudge us, and if God doesn't lead us in a particular situation, we can often let go. I'm not saying that we speak of Christ only when we feel nudged. Ultimately, as we are true to ourselves and our identity as followers of Christ, we will *often* have opportunities to express our identity and our experiences. So we take whatever opportunity comes our way. But as we are going and speaking of the good news and being who we are, learning to listen to God's Spirit may be the most transformational habit we can acquire.

THE HOLY SPIRIT DETECTIVE AGENCY

Another great image to guide us in evangelism today is a detective agency. We are junior partners in the Holy Spirit Detective Agency. We look for clues. We ask good questions of our lead detective, the Holy Spirit, and of people. Where is God already at work?

Paul was great at pursuing evangelism as a spiritual detective. For instance, look at Paul in Athens, a story recorded in Acts 17. Paul explored Athens and found a sign of genuine spiritual interest and humility in the midst of a pagan and highly spiritually confused, faddish and intellectually prideful environment. He found an altar to an unknown God. It wasn't much to work with, but it was a clue. God was on the case.

If the Holy Spirit is the first and primary witness and we are junior partners collaborating with the Holy Spirit, how do we learn to see and hear what the Holy Spirit is up to? Three primary skills can help us.

First, we can listen to the whispers and nudges of the Holy Spirit to show us where God is at work in the lives of those around us.

Second, we can ask great questions of others to find clues for where God is already at work in their lives.

Third, we can collaborate with God in prayer *for* seekers and skeptics and *with* seekers and skeptics.

LISTENING TO THE HOLY SPIRIT

Our goal is to collaborate with God, believing that God is already working. So when I fly on a plane, take a taxi, play tennis with a friend, or buy a bagel at Einstein Bros. Bagels or Panera, I will often pause for a moment and ask God if there is something he is doing in somebody near me. Often I get no sense of anything and proceed about my business. But sometimes I feel nudged by God. And usually when I step out, I am encouraged. God is often at work and wants to work with and through me. I am not the one who creates the opportunities or makes it all happen.

My friend Yreille from the Bahamas has learned this practice. She is often out in the community, looking for ways to serve and care for people. As she reaches out, she asks God to show her where God is at work.

God gave her a heart for one woman who was very closed. Every day on her way to work, Yreille would see this woman at the window of her home. Yreille would wave every day. At first, the woman would merely turn away. Over time, though, she began to wave back.

Next, Yreille took her some snacks she had made and left them with her, saying very little. Time went by. Finally, one morning Yreille sensed the Holy Spirit telling her it was time. So she knocked on the door, and when the woman opened it, Yreille told her that God wanted her to know this morning that he loved her, that he saw her pain and loneliness, and that God wanted to begin to change that in her life.

Suddenly this very stoic and unfriendly woman began to weep, and her heart began to melt. She gave her life to God. Later she told Yreille that she had been thinking about God that morning and wondering if God could help her and speak to her.

Yreille has worked a lot in the Bahamas and in Haiti, and she, like many in the developing world, has much to teach us about the Holy Spirit's ways. Yreille is not charismatic or Pentecostal, but she is sensitized to the voice of the Spirit. An author who has emphasized evangelism as listening and partnering with the Holy Spirit is York Moore in his book *Growing Your Faith by Giving It Away*. I take every opportunity I can to learn from such mentors, and this pursuit of collaboration with the Holy Spirit is becoming more and more a part of my life.

If I am honest, I must admit that sometimes I feel the nudge of the Holy Spirit but don't respond. Recently I passed a homeless man on the street. In the middle of conversation with my boss about an important issue, I felt that old familiar nudge to give this homeless man a buck and engage him in a bit of conversation. My boss would have understood; he loves witness too. But I didn't respond. I kept talking away about things that seemed important at the time, though I can't for the life of me remember what they were. Who knows where responding to that man could have led? As C. S. Lewis writes in *The Voyage of the "Dawn Treader,"* "We are never told what might have been."

If the Holy Spirit is the first and primary witness, seeing what the Holy Spirit is doing and collaborating with the Holy Spirit is crucial. When we are seeking to be a witness, there may be no other single thing we can do that will have greater impact than learning to listen to God. So how do we listen to the Holy Spirit? How do we know when the Spirit is nudging us or leading us?

The heart of the practice is learning to recognize that God is actually present with you and then to ask this very present God good questions. Then you wait until he speaks into your heart and mind. When I pray, first I focus my mind on God's presence by getting quiet and receptive for a moment. Then I regularly ask God good questions:

- Jesus, where are you already at work? Lord, lead me to people who are receptive.
- Is there someone you want me to talk to, care for or pray with? Is there someone here who is hurting?

Whenever I teach people about witness these days, a challenge I pose is for them to take an afternoon, or a lunchtime or another mealtime, and walk around just looking at people and listening to God. Instead of urging them to walk up to whoever they see and try to start a conversation, I encourage them to ask God to lead them particularly to someone in whom God is already at work. I am often amazed at the stories people come back with. They will have ministered to hurting people or talked with particularly open people. They get so excited by this vision of life and witness in collaboration with God.

One student, after reading John Teter's book *Get the Word Out* and receiving the same challenge to listen to God, started walking his dorm floors, asking the Holy Spirit to lead him. He went from floor to floor, seeing closed doors everywhere. Finally, on the last floor of the dorm, he saw an open door. He felt the nudge of God's Spirit to knock on the partly opened door to see who was there and what they were up to. He knocked, and those inside invited him in. He found three seeking and skeptical students arguing about the Bible! They were talking about whether the world was created or just happened, and for some reason they wanted to look up what the Bible had to say about creation. But they didn't have a Bible. So God sent them this student, Jason, who did have a Bible! He retrieved it, and the four of them spent an hour studying Genesis 1. Shades of Philip and the Ethiopian eunuch, as recorded in Acts 8!

God wants to lead us and connect us and use us in these powerful and collaborative ways far more than we have realized. Can you imagine what might happen if your church or fellowship group got committed and on fire for being filled and led by the Holy Spirit in this way?

ASKING GREAT QUESTIONS

The first habit we can cultivate, then, is asking God's Spirit good questions as we relate to the people around us. The second habit we can cultivate is learning to ask good questions of others to discover where God might be at work in their lives. What kinds of questions could help you know where God is already at work in the lives of the people around you? We have been taught to focus on people's beliefs when we ask them questions: What do you believe about God? Who do you think Jesus is? Do you believe we are sinful? How do we become reconciled to God? What must we do to be saved? Unfortunately, people in post-Christian society aren't that interested in talking about their beliefs. Those questions don't really engage them, nor do they help you discover where God might be at work.

On the other hand, these days people are very interested in the spiritual dimension of life. They are fascinated by experiences of the spiritual and the uncanny. Many popular movies have a strong spiritual or at least occult dimension. Think of the Matrix trilogy, *The Lord of the Rings*, the Harry Potter books and movies, the movies of M. Night Shyamalan, and the unexpected success of Mel Gibson's *The Passion of the Christ*. People want to share their experiences, hear your experiences and talk about spiritual reality.

As in Athens at the time of Paul's visit two centuries ago, there is much in this spiritual faddishness that is self-absorbed and hedonistic and unhelpful when it comes to knowing the real God, and bowing before God. But like Paul, we need to look for whatever is positive and build on that. So here are some questions that could help you find out what the Holy Spirit might be doing amid the mushrooming spiritual interest in our culture. Then, like Paul, you can affirm the good of the spiritual search and build on it, while still challenging self-absorbed spiritual faddishess.

- Do you have any religious background, and does it mean anything to you today?

- Have you ever had what you would consider a spiritual experience? What was that like?

- Have you ever had an experience of feeling close to God? What happened?

- Do you think there's a God? What do you think God might be like?

- What do you think about prayer? Do you think it works? What do you think it does?

Notice how experience focused most of these questions are. People will want to engage first at the level of their experience, not at the level of your beliefs about God, Jesus, sin and salvation.

Of course, at times we will need to challenge unhealthy spiritual fads too. We will explore ways to challenge the self-absorbed tenor of much contemporary spirituality in the chapter "Jesus Outside the Box."

In addition to asking these good starter questions, the heart of the process is inviting people to talk about their spiritual journey in the ways that they understand it. We want them to tell their stories. As they tell their stories, they will give us clues about how God is already at work.

- When have you experienced turning points and crises?

- What have you done with the spiritual side of life?

- Where do you seek perspective and help with your inner questions, doubts and struggles?

You could say something like this: "I think that probably everybody is concerned about the spiritual part of life in some way. So I like to ask people how they would describe their own spiritual journey. I know that's a personal question, but how would you describe your experience with the spiritual side of life?"

COLLABORATING WITH GOD IN PRAYER

In John 14, Jesus makes a startling promise:

> Don't you believe that I am in the Father, and that the Father is in me? The words I say to you are not just my own. Rather, it is the Father, living in me, who is doing his work. Believe me when I say that I am in the Father and the Father is in me; or at least believe on the evidence of the miracles themselves. I tell you the truth, anyone who has faith in me will do what I have been doing. He will do even greater things than these, because I am going to the Father. And I will do whatever you ask in my name, so that the Son may bring glory to the Father. You may ask me for anything in my name, and I will do it.

Notice, the secret of the miracles and the power of the prayers was once again this dynamic of collaboration. Jesus did what he did because he and the Father were one. The Father was living in him and doing the works. In our case, the Father and the Son have made their home in us by the Spirit (John 14:23). Witness and prayer are not first of all our work; they are God's work in us and through us. In witness and prayer, Another lives in us, and we are the junior partners.

As a result, the potential is there for us to do what Jesus did and even greater things. This potential largely goes unrealized, but every step toward it will transform our meager little efforts into Holy Spirit-empowered witness and prayer.

The crucial part is learning to pray in Jesus' name, which means according to the character of Jesus and in union with him. Romans 8:34 tells us that Jesus intercedes for us at God's right hand, and Romans 8:26-27 tells us that the Spirit intercedes for us with sighs too deep for words and according to the will of God. In prayer, we enter into God's prayers. Our prayers are most powerful when they are a participation in the prayers of the Son and the Spirit.

How do we participate in the prayers of the Son and the Spirit? Let's break this question down into two questions:

1. How do we pray *for* seeking and skeptical people?

2. How do we pray *with* seeking and skeptical people?

First, we need to note that there are certain prayers God will not answer when we pray for seeking and skeptical people. Any prayer that would lead to a violation of people's freedom to choose or reject God will not be answered. God will not violate our freedom to choose. God wants love or nothing; forced allegiance is not part of God's will. This truth is agonizing for those of us with friends, family and especially children who do not yet follow Jesus. Every bone in our body and every cell in our being wants some way to enforce their commitment to Jesus. But prayer was never intended to be a means of control, either over God or over others. The essence of prayer is humility, a recognition of our limits, helplessness and powerlessness. In that sense, prayer is powerful to the degree that we recognize our own helplessness and neediness.

There is no easy answer or simple comfort to give when loved ones, and especially one's children, reject Jesus or are apathetic. But we can pray that God will be active in pursuit and that God will bring followers of Jesus into their lives to love them, reach out to them and speak truth to them. No parent has suffered more agony over lost and wandering children than God has. So take comfort and don't feel swallowed up by a sense of failure. You're in good company. God knows what it's like to have children who reject the faith of their parents.

Here is a brief but dynamic list of prayers that Scripture shows us God will bless and empower. They are prayers we can pray in participation with God and in line with God's will.

- God's presence and power for witness: Luke 24:49; Acts 1:4, 8, 14; 2:2-4

- oneness in the body of Christ: John 17:21-23

- sanctification and strengthening for us: Ephesians 6:13; 1 Thessalonians 5:23-24

- boldness: Acts 4:29

- miracles/healing/prophecy: Acts 4:30; 1 Corinthians 14:24

- guidance and wisdom, divine appointments: Acts 8:26-40; Colossians 4:2

- conviction of seekers: John 16:8-11

- peace so that the gospel can spread: 1 Timothy 2:1-4, 8

- discernment and the gift of battle against the ways the enemy has blinded the minds of unbelievers: 2 Corinthians 4:4; Ephesians 6:10-13, 18-20

- that lost ones whom we love may be saved (though notice that this prayer involves free choice and often went unanswered for Paul—nevertheless, God wants us to put our desires into prayers!): Romans 10:1

- colaborers in witness: Matthew 9:35-38

Just as powerful as praying *for* seekers and skeptics, we can also, and especially these days, pray *with* seekers and skeptics.

We often pray for physical healing for people already in God's family, and sometimes God answers those prayers. But actually I have more often seen God work powerfully in prayers for physical healing for my seeking friends. I find biblical precedents for this in Jesus' ministry and in the book of Acts.

My friend Sam works at Einstein Bros. Bagels, where I write my books. Sam has a Muslim dad and a kind-of-Baptist mom. Recently, as I was going through the line, Sam waved me over. "I've lost my wallet again. I don't know where it is!"

"Sam, I will pray for you to find it," I assured him.

"I guess it can't hurt," he replied. (I get that response a lot.)

Ten minutes later, he came over and told me he had found it. "All right!" I rejoiced. "Hey, you can ask me to pray for you anytime." He laughed.

The next week as I went through the line, Sam let me know his ulcer was acting up. "Sam, is there anything I can get you?" I asked. He sent me over to the nearby grocery store to pick up some medicine. When I came back, I told him I would pray too. This time he welcomed my prayers a little more enthusiastically.

Ten minutes later, he approached me and said he felt much better and hadn't needed to take the medicine. That was very unusual for him.

"Man, I wish I had prayed for you before I went and bought that medicine!" I exclaimed. He laughed again.

These days he doesn't wait for me to ask. When I see Sam, he often asks me to pray for him without any suggestion from me at all. I feel like his personal priest!

God seems to love to answer these kinds of prayers for Sam more than God seems to want to answer those kinds of prayers for me. God wants to make tangible his rule and authority and power, especially where people are not following him. I think God has a different priority for me. God wants a deeper maturity from me and a love that is not dependent on being steered to good parking places and being healed of my sniffles or even of more serious illnesses. But God's Spirit seems to love to meet seekers and skeptics where they are and to stretch out his hand to minister, even miraculously, whenever they ask. And we get to collaborate with the Holy Spirit.

When is it appropriate to pray with our seeking friends? Whenever I have a little deeper conversation with someone who isn't a Christ follower and he has been honest about his needs, if I am in a place where I can pray with him without drawing attention, I will ask if I can do that. You can too.

CONCLUSION

The Holy Spirit is the first and primary witness. We are junior partners called to collaborate. As we listen to God, ask great questions, watch for clues of God at work, and pray with and for seekers and skeptics, our witness can be transformed. What a Holy Spirit adventure!

3

THE WITNESS OF THE COMMUNITY

Cindy was a skeptic who attended her first Alpha meeting only because she was dragged there. Alpha is a ten-week course for seekers and skeptics that begins with a banquet whose theme is "Christianity: Boring, Untrue and Irrelevant?" Her friend Paula had participated in an earlier Alpha course and become a follower of Jesus. She would be telling her story that first night, and she begged and pleaded for Cindy to come to provide moral support. Cindy couldn't think of a good way to say no, and so she went.

Later, in discussion around tables, Cindy admitted she wasn't sure why she was there. She had a lot of doubts about faith and couldn't see herself "doing the Christian thing."

Brock spoke up. He agreed with her. He wasn't sure why he was there, and had planned on not saying a word. But he so identified with Cindy's feelings. You could feel the intense energy between Cindy and Brock. Cindy later remarked, "How cool! I thought I would come to a Christian meeting and be told what to believe. Instead, I was affirmed for my doubts and questions and lack of belief. I loved it!"

Brock and Cindy both continued to attend every week. Each week, they shared doubts and questions, and over the weeks, ironically, each was the other's most crucial influence in keeping them coming to learn more about Jesus! As they voiced honest questions to one another and to others, and as they experienced being in a safe place where they could belong without believing, the Holy

Spirit was free to work very powerfully in their lives.

Halfway through Alpha, the group went on a retreat together. Brock almost dropped out at the last minute, but Cindy got him to come. They were both intrigued by the teaching about the Holy Spirit. When it came time for a ministry session Saturday night on the retreat, Cindy, who had been struggling with thoughts of suicide, received prayer for depression and experienced a gift of joy. That experience influenced Cindy to become more positive and intentional in her spiritual search. And Cindy's change influenced Brock. Cindy can't point to a moment, but she knows that somewhere during those months of attending Alpha, she came to faith and trust in God.

Cindy told her story at the next Alpha kickoff banquet, just as Paula had at the previous banquet. And she made sure Brock was there to listen. As Brock listened to her story, in which he played such a central role, his heart began to melt, and from then on he became a much more intentional seeker. He too later discovered that he had come to believe somewhere along the way.

Who led Brock and Cindy into becoming Christ-followers? Besides the Holy Spirit, and each other as skeptical seekers, there was a whole team, a whole community, at work.

There was Peter. He was a good administrator, and he and his wife were gifted in hospitality. They set just the right tone of welcome for each meeting.

There was Lou. He could tell a great joke and didn't seem like your typical "holy roller" Christian. Any moment, you expected him to pop the top on a six-pack or light up a smoke. He was just that kind of guy.

There was Hope. She loved creating beautiful spaces, and she loved providing good food. She was a gifted connector, often working behind the scenes to bring people together over a good meal or a fun event.

There was Neel. She was a good storyteller and teacher, able to make biblical truths practical and concrete. You just liked her and enjoyed listening to her. She made every week's teaching session personal and helpful.

And there were Chris and Molly. They were married and loved leading small groups. They knew how to ask good questions, affirm people for whatever they said and speak truth out of their own life experiences. When they got particularly off-the-wall comments from seekers or skeptics in the group, they didn't lose their cool. "That's very interesting," one of them would respond. "What do others think?"

Finally, there was Wes. He prayed for Cindy on Saturday night at the retreat. He sensed the Spirit nudging him to pray for a past traumatic relationship with a boyfriend, and God ministered to Cindy in a very deep way. Her depression lifted, and she left looking radiant.

The only person in the whole group who thought he might have the gift of evangelism was Wes. And even he felt he wasn't very good at it. Yet God used this community of people as the channel of the Holy Spirit to lead Cindy and Brock to faith. This story, I believe, captures the shape of witness in a post-Christian world.

WHY COMMUNITY?

Most people today will come to faith in the context of a community. Belonging comes before believing. Evangelism today is about helping people belong so that they can come to believe.

There are a number of reasons for this shift to a central focus on community in the process of conversion, but none may be as important as the parallel shift from a culture in which Protestant faith is dominant to a culture that is postmodern and post-Christian.

The values and beliefs of our culture have become more pagan and less Christian. Jay Leno has done a great job of uncovering the growing biblical illiteracy in his roving interviews on the streets. People today often don't know the Ten Commandments, what the Sermon on the Mount is, who the apostles were, or what words like *God, sin* and *salvation* mean in a biblical sense. And here is the great irony. Although people today know less about Christian faith than they used to, they think they know what it is and have decided they don't want it.

In the movie *Sister Act,* Whoopi Goldberg, as a youngster about to be kicked out of Catholic school, is asked to name the twelve apostles. She gets one: John. Then she goes to Paul. He wasn't one of the Twelve, but at least he was an apostle. Pausing for a few moments, she nails the next two—George and Ringo (of the Beatles)! Her answers are funnier than most people's, but she also probably gets more names right than many people today would.

The Judeo-Christian language and worldview can no longer be assumed. Therefore, the conversion process takes longer and requires learning the language, concepts and identity of being Christian. This kind of learning can take place only in community.

In the past, we had a very individualistic and rational concept of the conversion process. We gave people the right information and called for an immediate decision. Then, after they committed themselves to faith, we would invite them to join the community for discipleship. Now we understand that the community needs to be the context for the conversion process all the way along.

Whenever people embrace a new identity—a transformation

that is at the heart of conversion—they are embracing the community that makes that identity possible. And with that comes adoption of the language and conceptual framework that constitute this community. Identity, community, language and conceptual framework are all so interrelated that you cannot separate their roles in the conversion process. Conversion involves joining a community, learning a language and adopting a worldview. None of these dimensions operates in isolation. You either get them all together or get none of them at all.

Words like *God, prayer, devotion, worship, confession, obedience* and all the other ways we talk about and live out our faith mean nothing when divorced from the practices of the community that give those words meaning. Conversion involves learning the language and corresponding practices that constitute Christian identity. In that sense, the conversion process and the discipleship process are the same. *Conversion* is merely the term we use for a good beginning, a good imitation.

When we could assume a largely nominal Protestant culture, many words like *God, prayer, worship, Scripture* and even *sin* had widely shared definitions. In that context evangelists could emphasize the few missing pieces and call for conversion. Today the process is longer and takes much more teaching. Conversion today is more like learning a second language from scratch. Such language learning can take place only in genuine Christian community.

The seeker church movement took the practices of itinerant evangelists like Billy Graham and made them part of the ongoing life of the local church. That way, people could learn the language in the context of a community. Yet today the megachurches that resulted may not be the ideal places for language learning. There is a very strong movement back toward smaller churches, partly because the learning of the language and practices of a genuine Christian identity now needs very personalized and intimate connection and community. Many megachurches have kept pace by meeting these needs for intimacy and language learning through believer small groups, seeker small groups and recovery groups.

Whenever the church has needed to reach pagan or non-Christian cultures, the community has been primary in the process of conversion. How do we involve people in community where they can belong before they have to believe?

First, we can invite unchurched people to activities and events that are designed to be entry points into the community. Alpha, seeker small groups, vacation Bible school, movie and book discussion groups, Christmas teas and parties, special services aimed at seekers, and marriage enrichment and divorce and addiction recovery seminars all help unchurched people enter into the community and belong before they have to believe. Ideally, these entry points are more than onetime occasional events. People today need regular opportunities to connect and explore.

Second, we can invite unchurched people to events and efforts that serve the poor and work for justice and reconciliation. People today are especially drawn to ministries and people that are genuinely concerned for the poor and for reconciling broken relationships. And God has always been concerned for these things!

Axis is the Generation X (twentysomething) ministry of Willow Creek Church. Its most effective outreach event ever was when Shane Claiborne was invited to speak. Shane had interned with Mother Teresa, and at the time of the event he worked in Philadelphia with the homeless. The interview was a "buzz weekend"—one of three or four times a year when Axis folks work to bring in new people and follow it up well.

Shane spoke of his time with Mother Teresa. Mother Teresa had really deformed feet and legs, he said, because every time new shoes and socks came in and her sisters would give her a new pair, she would meet somebody in need and would give her shoes and socks away almost immediately. So she constantly wore shoes that distorted her feet.

That story touched people's hearts at Axis. At the end of the service, one Axis leader stood and said, "We want to challenge you to take a step to respond to what you've heard. Shane told us that one of the greatest needs of the poor is for shoes and socks. For those of us willing, let's leave our shoes and socks in back. I know we didn't prepare, but we just want to respond."

He and the other organizers expected maybe fifty pairs. By the end of it all, nine hundred pairs of shoes and socks were piled up in the back of the auditorium! I was there, and I walked out of the room blown away by how transforming faith can be. That event created belonging before believing, as seekers and believers both responded from their hearts. That event rocked the larger Willow world too. The church includes quite a few corporate types who, though comfortable with being casual, had some concerns about all those young people walking around in their bare feet!

Most church leaders think about compassion and serving the poor in very individualistic ways, for example through one-on-one tutoring and mentoring relationships. These avenues are good. But it is also very good to think in terms of community as you serve the poor and seek reconciliation. InterVarsity Christian Fellowship has been doing this each March when we send hundreds of students on spring-break projects to build homes for the poor with Habitat for Humanity. The only prerequisite for being involved is bringing along a seeking or skeptical friend. During the days, we build homes for and with the poor. Then each night, we offer Bible studies exploring Jesus' concern for the poor. Many churches could do the same kind of thing—for instance, by bringing seekers and skeptics along on mission trips. I realize there are issues to sort through in relation to this possibility; some churches may not feel comfortable sending seekers and skeptics to do "missions work." Those churches need to find other ways for people to be able to belong before they have to believe.

THE GIFTS OF THE HOLY SPIRIT

The witness of the Holy Spirit takes place not only *in* community, as we have been exploring, but also *through* community. The Holy Spirit works in witness through the diversity of spiritual gifts that God has given us.

One reason we feel guilty about our lack of evangelism, and tired when we think about doing evangelism, is that we tend to have a very individualistic concept of our responsibility. Most of us assume that if we got serious about sharing our faith, we would need to build friendships, talk to strangers, have people in our homes for meals and social events, study the Bible with un-churched people, explain the gospel, call them to Christ and then follow them up. We think we have to do it all. This pervasively individualistic viewpoint colors our thoughts about every Christian responsibility, not just witness.

The biblical viewpoint is fundamentally different. The writers of Scripture thought more in terms of *corporate* witness. Each of us, filled with the Holy Spirit, does our part to live like Jesus and minister in Jesus' name. Together, we contribute according to the gifts the Spirit gives us. That's the way the New Testament talks about all ministries, including ministry to seekers and skeptics.

In the New Testament, the call to become witnessing communities is much more central and important than the call to become witnessing individuals. There are very few commands in the New Testament for individuals to evangelize. We are all called to be able to "give a reason for the hope that is within us," whenever we are asked. Paul also asks the churches to pray always for his ministry of proclamation as an apostle. So we are called to pray for those who are especially gifted in evangelism. But beyond that, our primary responsibility is to take our place in the body of Christ and contribute to the witness of the church according to the gifts of the Spirit we have been given.

As Paul teaches us:

> We have different gifts, according to the grace given us. If a man's gift is prophesying, let him use it in proportion to his faith. If it is serving, let him serve; if it is teaching, let him teach; if it is encouraging, let him encourage; if it is contributing to the needs of others, let him give generously; if it is leadership, let him govern diligently; if it is showing mercy, let him do it cheerfully. (Romans 12:6-8)

Paul's words imply two questions each of us must answer:

1. What is your spiritual gift?

2. What is your measure of faith?

Use your spiritual gift according to your measure of faith. This challenge is applicable to every area of our involvement in our church, including witness. Your most important contribution to witness, in fact, lies in your area of gifting.

If you hear from God well and pray for others effectively, that's your area of greatest contribution to the witness of your community. If you are an encourager, that is your greatest area of contribution to the witness of your community.

If you are an evangelist and are especially gifted at leading people into a commitment to Jesus, that gift will be your greatest area of contribution to the witness of your community.

If you have a gift of hospitality, that will be your area of greatest contribution to the witness of your community.

If you are a great administrator and organizer, that will be your greatest area of contribution to the witness of the community.

Do you get the idea? What is your spiritual gift? How can your spiritual gift best contribute to the witness of your community?

I want to say a special word to leaders here. It is your unique role to lead the whole church or ministry into this vision of corporate witness. If you don't set the pace, cast the vision, clarify the mission and help people contribute to the witness of your church, very few people will ever come to know Christ through your community. In positive terms, likely the most strategic and transforming thing you could do as a leader is to help your church define, strategize and implement a vision for corporate witness in your community.

You don't have to be gifted in evangelism in order to lead your church into evangelism. You only have to be gifted in leadership. That's your spiritual gift. You have to be like Timothy, that relatively young, inexperienced and insecure pastor/teacher whom Paul calls to "do the work of an evangelist" (2 Timothy 4:5). Timothy was primarily a leader and teacher, but his role was to lead the whole community to engage in witness. So leaders, go ahead and lead. Lead your church or ministry into a corporate vision for witness, and help everyone find their role.

WORKING AS A BODY

Over the years, working with many different evangelism efforts, I have identified six key gift areas that, when unleashed for evangelism, lead to a powerful witness of the community. The crucial step is helping people identify their gift and see how they can contribute to the witness of their Christian community, letting the Holy Spirit use them in their areas of gifting. If the church could grasp the way God wants to use the whole community to reach people through the gifts God has given, our pictures and practices of evangelism would be transformed and people would be set free.

Following are the areas of gifting, taken from Scripture and experience, that God seems to love to use to reach our world in teamwork for corporate witness.

1. *Organizing and leading.* The key question for people who have gifts of organizing and leading, including the gift of administration, is, *How am I helping the whole community do the work of evangelism through my gifts of leadership?* This gift area is mentioned both in Romans 12:8 and in 1 Corinthians 12:28. Leaders paint the vision for vital witness by the community, lead the process of generating corporate strategy in witness, and help everyone find their gifts and contribution to the witness of the community.

2. *Evangelism and equipping.* The key question for evangelism equippers is, *How am I using my gift in evangelism to help others get in the game?* This gift area is mentioned in Ephesians 4:11. Notice that this gift area is grouped with the other leadership gifts of apostle, prophet and pastor/teacher and that the main purpose for these leadership gifts is equipping the saints for works of service. If you are an evangelist in the Ephesians 4 sense, of course you will witness personally, but even more, you will help others into witness. Too often when churches or ministries look for a point person for

evangelism, they seek out people who are good at sharing their faith but don't consider whether they are good at helping others share their faith. We need evangelism *leaders* and *equippers* to lead the charge and help us all get in the game. If you are such an evangelism leader, you are a crucial part of the team, motivating and training others in witness. Often you will be the person who best understands the questions of seekers and skeptics and is most energized by answering those questions in credible and persuasive ways. Finally, you may also be highly motivated to invite people to become followers of Jesus at the right moment in their journey.

3. *Hospitality and encouragement.* The key question for people with gifts in hospitality and encouragement is, *How am I reaching out to people outside the church through hospitality and encouragement?* This gift area is mentioned in Romans 12:8-13. Hospitality and encouragement are possibly the most crucial initial gifts when it comes to rebuilding the broken trust of people in post-Christian cultures. People with gifts in encouragement and hospitality are very aware of whether others are comfortable and fitting in. These gifts are crucial in the first stages of building the sense of community that God can use in the lives of seekers today.

4. *Pastoring and teaching.* The key question for pastor/teachers is, *How I am using my relational and teaching gifts in the lives of seekers and skeptics?* This gift area is mentioned in Romans 12:7, 1 Corinthians 12:29 and Ephesians 4:11. It is in the last mention that pastoring and teaching are combined and classed with the other leadership gifts aimed at equipping the whole church. Pastor/teachers are especially crucial for leading small groups in any community's witness and also for speaking to groups that include seekers and skeptics. Since people today need a place to connect before they commit and a safe place to ask their questions and ex-

press their doubts, small groups are probably the centerpiece for most church witness in the contemporary world. Thus people with some relational skill and the ability to lead lively, instructive discussion sessions become key players in a community's strategy for witness.

5. *Prayer, words and works from the Holy Spirit.* The crucial question for people with gifts in the area of prayer and prayer ministry is, *How are my prayer gifts being used in ministry to seekers and skeptics?* This gift area is mentioned especially in 1 Corinthians 12:7-10, 28-31, but also in Romans 12:6 and Ephesians 4:11 (prophets). People today are very interested in spiritual experiences and long to know through personal experience that God is real. Our culture is becoming more pagan and spiritualistic, and so healing and words from the Holy Spirit, ministered to people through prayer, are becoming an even more crucial part of the spiritual journey.

6. *Service and mercy.* The key question for those with this gift area is, *How are my gifts of service and mercy helping build trust for the gospel with those who don't know Jesus?* This gift area is mentioned in Romans 12:7-8 and 1 Corinthians 12:28 (those able to help others). Ministries of compassion and justice and service to people in need are the most important kinds of evidence for the genuineness of the gospel in a world that is tired of words and marketing. People today will know God is real as our message is lived out and makes a difference. Those with gifts in service and mercy build trust by their own service and also can help all of us by calling us to service and compassion with the poor.

My experience shows that this set of gifts, brought together in a team context, makes for powerful witness through community. If you have a leader/administrator, a trainer/motivator, a hospitality person, a good small group leader, a prayer person and a service/

compassion person, you have a high-impact team.

What if you don't have all those gifts and people? Start with what you have and ask God to give you what you still need.

A final gift often works behind the scenes but plays a crucial empowerment role.

7. *Giving.* The key question for givers is, *How is my giving helping the whole church reach the unchurched?* This gift area is mentioned in Romans 12:8. In Philippians 4:14-19 Paul lets the Philippians know how by partnering with him as an apostle, they had brought inexpressible joy and encouragement to his heart. As givers, you have the discernment to recognize a good investment and the capacity to bless and encourage the witness of the community. Use your gift, your generosity, to help the gospel ring out to those who don't know Jesus. What an opportunity you have!

BEING FILLED BY THE HOLY SPIRIT

Have you ever felt as if God wants more for you? Have you ever asked to be filled with the Holy Spirit, and anointed in new ways for ministry and witness? Have you ever asked God to use your spiritual gifts in witness?

James tells us that "you do not have, because you do not ask God" (James 4:3). In Luke, Jesus tells us, "How much more will your Father in heaven give the Holy Spirit to those who ask him!" (Luke 11:13). And Paul challenges Timothy to "fan into flame the gift of God, which is in you through the laying on of my hands" (2 Timothy 1:6).

Saints throughout the ages testify to the need to ask. Dwight L. Moody, that great nineteenth-century evangelist, spent years restless and dissatisfied with a sense of fruitlessness and a lack of fullness of the Holy Spirit. After the Chicago fire in 1871, when Moody lost his great buildings, he came to the end of himself. Burned out, discouraged and with no heart for ministry, Moody found himself crying out to God while walking the length of Wall Street in New York City. God met him and filled him. He later wrote, "Ah, what a day!—I cannot describe it, I seldom refer to it, it is almost too sacred to name—Paul had an experience of which he never spoke for fourteen years—I can only say God revealed himself to me, and I had such an experience of His love that I had to ask Him to stay His hand." A friend later reported Moody's awareness that "God blessed him with the *conscious* incoming to his Soul of a presence and power of His Spirit such as he had never known before." He looked back on that event as the decisive moment in his empowering for fruitfulness and broad impact.

To consider a more contemporary example: Pete Greig, the founder of the 24/7 prayer movement and leader in Culture Shift, a network of people experimenting with church in the emerging culture, speaks of exactly the same kind of fresh and deeper empowering. "Standing on the spectacular cliffs of St. Vincent, on the southwestern point of Europe," Greig reminisces, "I had no idea that my life was about to change." He goes on to tell of an infilling of the Holy Spirit and a vision of young people raised up in every nation to pray and labor for the gospel. The 24/7 prayer movement came out of that infilling. It consists of prayer rooms, called boiler rooms, practicing around-the-clock prayer in a pattern established by the Moravians a few centuries ago. Its heartbeat is intimacy with Jesus through the fullness of the Spirit.

We may not be gifted for Moody's or Greig's level of leadership and influence, but every one of us needs deeper and consistent infusions of the presence and power of God's Spirit. And many of us have never even asked to be filled and empowered in those ways.

How about you? Have you ever asked for this consciously experienced infilling of the Holy Spirit to set free your spiritual gifts in the service of others? Will you seek and knock, going to those whose ministries seem to be empowered by God's Spirit and seeking God's filling through a laying on of hands? So often we think of being filled by the Spirit in the same individualistic way we think about life and ministry in general. We ask God privately and individually. But God works through the community and the laying on of hands to fill people with the Spirit. Will you ask to be filled with God's Spirit? Will you ask God for a team or witnessing community through which you can contribute your part to reaching people who don't know God?

4

THE ART OF SPIRITUAL FRIENDSHIP

Daniel worked with a twentysomething ministry at a large church. As time passed, he began to feel increasingly frustrated that all his friends were church friends. He didn't have any spiritual friends who didn't already know and follow Jesus. One day, sitting in a Starbucks, he cried out to God. "God, where can I find some people for whom I could become a friend on the spiritual journey? Where do people of my generation congregate? Where can I find people spiritually interested but far from God?" At that moment, Daniel had an epiphany. He looked around and realized his generation worked at Starbucks. Here were lots of people who were from his generation and who were largely unchurched.

So he asked God to help him develop some friendships at Starbucks. What he sensed from God in response to his prayer surprised him. He felt nudged by God not just to hang out at Starbucks, drink coffee and build trust but to get a job at Starbucks and develop some spiritual friendships up close and personal, as a coworker.

He returned to his supervising pastor and asked for time to work at Starbucks. To his surprise, she loved the idea. So with her blessing, off he went. What he learned at Starbucks changed his whole approach to sharing his faith.

THE STARBUCKS GENERATION

Daniel expected to begin working, spend a couple of months building trust, then share the gospel and begin baptizing people behind the espresso bar. He expected that all people needed was a relationship with a cool Christian and then a good explanation of the gospel. What he discovered in his friendships was very different.

One surprise was that all twenty-one people he worked with believed in God. Not one was an atheist. Their lives and attitudes and his impression of the broader culture had led him to expect many more people to be anti-God. But they were all very positive toward God and spirituality.

A second surprise was that all were very interested in spiritual things but not in Christians, Christianity or the church. No one wanted to hear Daniel's proofs for God or invitations to come to church or ideas about salvation. Almost everyone thought they knew what Christianity was about and had decided they didn't want it. They were post-Christian. At some point along the way, each of them had experienced a breach in trust related to Christianity. Maybe a Christian friend had been hypocritical or pushy. Maybe when they were young they had attended church and found it boring and irrelevant. Maybe they had watched TV preachers and been turned off. Or maybe they had experienced a tragedy—death or sexual abuse or some other trauma—and felt that God had been distant or uncaring.

Daniel still remembers vividly the day he asked a coworker about her feelings about a relationship with God. She looked at him and then blurted out, "I want to know where God was when I was fourteen and somebody raped me."

Daniel was stunned. What can you say at a moment like that? She had personally experienced a profound breach in trust with God.

For different people, the particular issue varied. But almost every one at Starbucks had experienced some breach in trust with

God or with Christians. So Daniel wasn't starting at ground zero, but rather at minus three or four. He would have to pierce through their stereotypes and rebuild broken trust before they would even listen to what he had to say.

Over a year and a half later, Daniel left Starbucks, having seen many changes. He had become the Starbucks priest, and his fellow workers had come to appreciate his role in their lives. They had learned to joke about spiritual things in healthy ways with Daniel. One day when he came to Starbucks, he'd found out that his co-workers were having a contest to see who could confess the most outrageous sin to him.

Along with these gains, Daniel's view of evangelism had been transformed. The biggest thing Daniel learned is that people in this generation have a prior question of trust that must be addressed before he can have meaningful spiritual conversations with them.

THE PRIOR QUESTION OF TRUST

I have redefined evangelism as conversations with friends on a spiritual journey. It is more like having a conversation on a journey than closing the deal on a sales call. We are travel guides, not traveling salespeople.

Today many people in our culture have a breach of trust with Christians, the church or God. Many people are post-Christian. They think they know what Jesus, the church and Christians are about, and they have decided they don't want them.

How do we rebuild the bridge of trust? How do we develop spiritual friendships in which genuine and transformational conversation can take place?

Here's a key: We get more committed to a *process* of spiritual friendship, and we focus on the Holy Spirit and what the Holy Spirit is up to instead of on some mental script about how the relationship and the conversation should unfold.

Does that mean we give up the desire to see our friends become followers of Jesus? Do we give up intentionality in spiritual friendships and spiritual conversations? Not at all. We just give up the *script* we have in our head for how it all ought to go. The dichotomy between being a genuine friend and intentionally acting to see people move toward God is a false dichotomy. If we care about people, we will want their best for every part of their lives, including the spiritual part.

DEVELOPING GENUINE FRIENDSHIPS

Genuine friendship starts with sharing common interests. What do you love to do? Watch baseball? Play video games? Study literature or write? Read books? Play chess? Sail boats? Play basketball? Go to movies? Cultivate flowers? The list could go on and on. Too often Christians don't spend enough time doing what they love to do. And too often they ignore the greatest opportunity for building friendships with people far from God. They don't do what they love to do—or they do what they love only with other Christians.

One of my friends at church, Michael, loves to play golf. He doesn't play golf to convert people. He plays golf because he loves to do it.

Mike loves to play golf with seekers and skeptics. He could choose to play golf only with other Christians. But he joins golfing threesomes and twosomes to get to know people who are far from God. He and another friend have decided that golfing with seekers and

skeptics is fun and stimulating and also serves a kingdom purpose.
Mike isn't constantly trying to evangelize while he's playing golf.
He's playing golf. But being a Christ-follower is the most important
element of his personal identity. So his faith comes out naturally at
some point during each golf game. He's a good golfer and a warm
person, so people who golf with Mike are influenced toward Jesus.
Many of us could "be like Mike"!

I also think of Bill Hybels, senior pastor of Willow Creek
Church. Every summer he sails a lot, as anybody who has heard
him speak knows well! He doesn't sail just to evangelize; he would
have sailed no matter what, because he loves sailing. But he
chooses to sail with seekers and skeptics rather than with Christians. People who sail with Bill become better sailors, *and* they are
influenced toward Jesus!

So spend a few moments getting creative. Ask yourself two questions.

1. *What do I love to do?*

2. *How could I do what I love with people who don't know Jesus yet?*

Simple questions. But they could change your life and give the
Holy Spirit new opportunities to use you in influencing the lives of
others.

As you develop genuine friendships, you will probably be surprised by what your greatest asset is. It's your humanity. It's your
weaknesses, doubts and questions. Most people today are not at
first interested in your answers. But they will immediately relate to
and identify with your questions and struggles. Are your kids ever
troubled? Do you ever have doubts about your own worth? Do you
struggle with your body image or with feelings of failure? Do you
have any regrets?

In the church we often think that our greatest strengths are our victories and successes. We don't even want to expose our faith to another unless we have things all together. In evangelism classes we spend much time training people to know the right answers but very little time teaching people to ask the right questions, of God, others and themselves. We've got it backwards. People will let us in if they feel we have shared their struggles. People will identify with our humanity if we will share it.

These days, identification comes before influence. People aren't interested in our answers unless they feel we have the same questions and struggles they do. Being human is much more important than being an expert!

Your greatest strengths for evangelism, then, are already present:

- what you love to do
- what you struggle with, doubt and question

What are your greatest barriers to evangelism?

- having few or no genuine spiritual friendships with unchurched people
- having a mental script about "proper" evangelism that keeps you from sharing your struggles and collaborating with what God is actually doing in the lives of your spiritual friends

If you've been a Christian for years, you probably have very few genuine friendships with people far from God. Most of us long-time believers are in that boat.

And if you've been taught evangelism or just picked it up from those around you, you probably have a script for what to say and how conversations ought to go—and it may keep you from seeing how God is at work. We have been taught to direct evangelistic conversations in ways that undermine our friendships and close our eyes to the genuine spiritual journey of those around us.

Let me tell you about my own fork in the road in relation to these two barriers. During my attendance at a private college in eastern Pennsylvania, I became a small group leader in our campus fellowship group. As a small group leader, I led a Bible study, attended weekly leaders' meetings, met weekly with my coleader (a woman I was dating!) to prepare for the small group, met weekly with a couple of younger high-potential leaders in the group to mentor them, attended large group gatherings, went to church on Sunday, had daily Bible study and prayer, and attended a weekly prayer meeting. In addition, I carried a full load as an engineering student.

You may be a student and have a similar list, or you may be working and have a similar set of commitments to family and church. Here was the bottom line: when I got all done with all my many Christian activities and friendships, I was full up. I had very little time to do anything fun that I loved and that wasn't religious. And I was not doing anything that I loved with people who were far from God.

John Stott, the well-known Christian author, might have called me a rabbit-hole Christian, running from holy huddle to holy huddle. I would not have seen it that way. I was just a typical Christian involved in all the many events and activities of my Christian group.

I will never forget the Friday night I got off the frenetic bus of Christianity-ism and did something I loved with someone far from God. I skipped our regular large group gathering to go skiing with the ski club. That evening I hung out with a fellow fraternity brother named Scott.

Scott and I took to the slopes of Camelback Mountain. I remember trying to use the script in my head to talk to him. I posed several awkward questions—for one, I asked Scott if he had ever considered whether there might be a Designer or Artist behind all the natural beauty and order around us. I asked the question fairly incoherently, stumbling over my words, because I was still trying to get the script right in my head. Scott just looked at me blankly and went on to something else.

I especially remember how I tried to bring up the incredible intricacies of the human body and point out that it just didn't seem logical that it all evolved by chance. Scott looked at me like I was talking some other language. He wasn't mean about it. He just couldn't make heads or tails of what I was saying. I felt so awkward that I fell down coming off the lift. I looked like Frosty the Snowman. It suddenly hit me how humorous it was that just after talking about the marvelous design of the human body, I had tripped and fallen flat on my face.

I finally stopped trying to figure out clever ways to start a spiritual conversation and just asked him straight up if he ever thought about God, what he thought, and whether he thought God cared about our little lives. He paused a moment and replied that lately he had been thinking about God and spiritual stuff a lot and wondering if the Bible could help him. He invited me to study the Bible with him!

The issue wasn't clever words. The issue was assuming that God was involved somehow and asking Scott to tell me in his own words how. That night began for me the great adventure of doing what I love to do (skiing) with people who don't know Jesus yet.

Back on campus, I met with the leader of the campus fellowship group, who had noticed I was missing from Friday's meeting. He wondered why. When I told him I skipped out to ski with some people who didn't know Jesus yet, it was clear he didn't know quite what to say. He was uncomfortable with skipping "church" to do something fun like skiing. Once you skipped church to go skiing, where would it end? Where would you draw the line? You might spend all your time skiing and watching movies and going hiking and almost never go to church! (And indeed that may be a danger for some, but probably not for you who are reading this book!)

At the same time, hanging out with people far from God was just what he had been encouraging us to do—although I'm not sure he ever took time to do it.

DO WHAT YOU LOVE

For what it's worth, I want to give you full encouragement and permission to skip some church activities and go do something that you love with people who don't know Jesus yet!

If you are a pastor or another kind of Christian leader, the best thing you could do is skip some church stuff (or cancel some church stuff!) to do fun stuff and be with people far from God. Maybe nothing else would refresh and refuel you like doing what you love and being with people who aren't churchy. If you would do it, your people would do it. I know it's threatening to think about encouraging people to skip some church activities. But we Christians are ingrown and parochial and overwhelmingly stressed out by our busyness—working, attending church, being with church friends and family, and taking ourselves way too seriously all along the way.

So coach baseball for your kids (if that's fun for you). Or golf every week. Attend plays. Join a writing group. Take a course that interests you. Join a fly fishing club or a fantasy league or a video club or a bridge group or a ski club. Do something you love—and don't do it just with church friends or in a church league. Have fun with people who don't yet know Jesus.

Christians often tell me that they just don't have time to add anything else to their stressed-out life. They feel guilty because they don't have any spiritual friendships with people far from God, so they feel like they're supposed to add another responsibility, or they carry the guilt of falling short once again in their Christian duty. You feel guilty because you are not fulfilling your Christian duty of having more fun? How crazy is that?

Jettison it all! Now if your intention is to build a friendship just to convert people, forget it. You won't feel genuine, and the other person won't like being your project. But if you need a good time and want to let go of your burdens for a while, just do it! And find a way to do what you love with some people who are outside the church. Many of them are more into having fun than we are, not so serious about themselves.

It is important to dispel one misconception people may have about what I am saying. Obviously God wants those of us who follow Jesus to live like Jesus. Jesus hung out all the time with sinners and tax collectors and party people like Levi, who seemed to know a lot more about having fun than the religious types did. But Jesus was also *different from* the people he hung out with. He certainly wasn't hung up on rules, but he was filled with love and had fun in ways that still honored God and God's ways. Yes, God still wants saints, people set apart to God. But God wants human saints, not plaster saints.

You may not be at a point where you can skip church activities and party with the pagans—you might find yourself becoming a pagan if you partied with the pagans! Certain situations or environments influence you too much. You certainly need to know your own limitations and to avoid any activities and experiences that pull you away from following Jesus. But you can still do something you love, and you can still do it with people who don't yet know Jesus.

STARTING SPIRITUAL CONVERSATIONS

Let's turn to our second weakness. We have a script that is more a barrier than a bridge to genuine spiritual conversation. How do we engage in spiritual conversations that are meaningful to us and to our spiritual friends?

How do we stay tuned to our friends and to the Holy Spirit at the same time? How do we discover what the Holy Spirit is doing in the lives of our friends? If we have jettisoned the script, then what do we turn to for guidance for sharing our faith with our friends?

I suggested earlier that rebuilding the bridge of broken trust is the greatest need for seekers and skeptics today. We live in a largely post-Christian society in which people do not trust Christians, the church or God; they think they know what Christianity is about, and they have decided that they don't want it. How do we rebuild the bridge of broken trust?

Jesus knew how to rebuild the bridge. One of the most inspiring and relevant spiritual encounters Jesus ever had was with a Samaritan woman at a well.

After a long day of ministry and traveling, Jesus sat by a well in Samaria. His followers had gone to a nearby town to get some fast food. Over the rise came a woman at the midpoint of the day to get water.

Seeing the woman, Jesus knew there were huge issues of broken trust that would form the backdrop of any conversation he would have with her. She was a woman. Jewish men didn't talk publicly with women. This woman expected Jesus to feel superior to her and to ignore her. The woman was a Samaritan too. Jews never talked to Samaritans. Samaritans were half-breed Gentile Jews. Their ancestors had been deported centuries before and had later returned with mixed blood and an impure religion. The Samaritan woman knew Jesus would probably feel superior about his ethnic and religious purity and background. The Samaritan woman also had a personal history, a checkered past. She had had five husbands, and the man she was living with was not her husband. She was coming to the well alone at noon, rather than with other women at the end of the day. Her social status was low; other Samaritan women apparently wouldn't even hang out and be seen with her. So the Samaritan woman probably expected to be ignored or judged or put down. She was very unlikely to have much trust and openness to Jesus.

Many unchurched people have similar fears that they will be judged, rejected and marginalized by church types if they enter into spiritual conversations. Jesus knew and understood the breach of trust he was facing.

If Jesus had launched right into a script about the Samaritan woman's need to become Jewish and convert, end of conversation. If Jesus had begun telling her she was a sinner who needed a Savior, conversation done—she expected that line of thought. If Jesus had ignored her because he didn't know what to say to a person with such huge trust issues, conversation never begun.

Instead Jesus did the unexpected, as you might expect! He did the one thing that would shock this woman out of her defended position behind the walls of past hurt. Jesus put himself in the place of neediness. He was thirsty. He asked her to help him. He broke the social rules and changed the social equation. He began to rebuild broken trust using his greatest asset, his humanity, his neediness.

We can follow Jesus in our witness. We can learn from his approach. If we will jettison our script and learn from Jesus, our witness can be unleashed in new and powerful ways. Following are several ideas, based on Jesus' approach, that could get us unstuck when we face huge issues of trust, as we often do in a post-Christian culture.

In spiritual friendships with people who don't know Jesus, *assume mistrust,* just as Jesus did. If we assume mistrust and seek to identify with broken trust and defuse it, we will discover unending opportunities for meaningful spiritual conversation.

It is very easy, in fact, to enter into spiritual conversations nowadays. As I mentioned earlier, I often hang out at a place called Einstein Bros. Bagels to do my writing. That place has become a little community for me.

One morning I was going through the line to get my coffee and chocolate-chip muffin. Raoul rang me up at the cash register. He and I had talked before. He had been intrigued when I told him what I do: "I hang out on campuses with spiritually interested people who are turned off by the organized church and by dogma." Today he asked again about how it was going.

Another worker, Jenny, toasting a cinnamon-raisin bagel, overheard Raoul ask me about helping spiritually interested people who were turned off by organized religion. Jenny was intrigued. From twenty feet away, with five people waiting to pay for their bagels and coffee, Jenny called out, "What was that? What do you do?"

I told her (and the five other people waiting) what I had told Raoul. She wanted to know how it was going. I explained, "I find a lot of people today who are spiritually interested but find the church kind of boring and irrelevant and religion kind of a turn-off. But they really want help on the spiritual journey from guides who won't judge them but will really care."

Jenny started to hyperventilate. "That's me! Where can I find people like that?" Jenny and I went on to have a twenty-minute spiritual conversation (after I got through the line!) that was meaningful and encouraging to both of us. By the end she was asking me for the names and locations of churches where she could have conversations like this one about her spiritual journey!

I used to think I couldn't even start a private conversation with people like Raoul, who have big trust issues with Christians and the church. Now I have confidence that as I wait on the Holy Spirit, I can talk to Raoul and simultaneously start a spiritual conversation with someone who is twenty feet away toasting bagels!

I also want to be honest with you. It's never easy for me to start conversations. I still feel the knot in the pit of my stomach and the "anxiety buzz" in my chest. Will the person respond? Will the conversation become awkward? Will I push them away, or will they reject me? And so I don't always take the risk when I see the opportunity or feel the nudge of the Spirit. But I wish I did because I have come to believe that the biggest thing I have to lose is the security of my comfort zone. And I have a lot to gain. My faith will grow, my God will be pleased, and my friend may make progress toward God.

I want you to notice something else about this conversation. Jenny and I had never talked before. Even if you have few relationships with friends who are not Christians, you may still have many opportunities for significant spiritual conversations, especially if you assume mistrust. In addition to assuming mistrust, *express your needs,* just as Jesus did. Don't feel as if you have to have it all together and convince the other person that you are practically perfect. When trust has been broken, leading with strength merely lengthens the distance between you and others. Broken trust is rebuilt as you show and share your humanity and your needs. An open, trusting heart is what melts the hearts and defuses the defenses of others.

An experience a couple of years ago really affected my understanding of witness. We were headed off on a family vacation, and a neighboring family had agreed to take care of our pets—a dog, two cats and a gerbil—while we were gone. The day before we were to leave, though, we found out that our cat was diabetic and would be needing shots twice a day. We went to the neighbors and said, "Hey, we'll put the cat with a vet, because we don't want you to have to shoot up our cat twice a day."

They responded, "No problem. We're glad to do it."

So off we went for two weeks. We came back, and indeed they had shot up our diabetic cat for two weeks. That was above and beyond. So we took them out to a nice Spanish tapas restaurant to thank them.

At the restaurant I had one of the most significant and profound spiritual conversations I have ever had. The man was a police commander and saw his spiritual vocation as providing pastoral and crisis care for police officers who had been involved in violence against others. He hadn't gone to church in years, but he was living out his calling. He and I opened up on a deep level, challenged each other and had a profound spiritual engagement. We continue to check in with each other and challenge each other to this day.

I thought about it later. What had so opened him up? Why were there no trust issues to overcome, even though he had had some negative experiences with the church and Christians? Why had he trusted me so much and so quickly? Then I realized what had built the trust. He had helped me when I needed it. He had been in the power position, because the helper always is. I was beholden to him. Nothing builds trust like being in a vulnerable receiving position with others.

I had been taught to practice "care evangelism," where I earn the right to be heard by caring for others. This experience taught me to pursue *mutual-care evangelism,* where I am seeking both to give *and* to receive as part of the relational and trust-building process.

As you reach out, look for opportunities both to serve and to ask for help. Your needs and your humanity are your greatest assets.

In spiritual friendships, *minister to wounded hearts,* just as Jesus did. The Samaritan woman had been wounded by the attitudes of Jews, wounded by the attitudes of men and wounded by her social isolation. Jesus asked her to meet his need and then conversed with her as a valuable and worthwhile person with good questions and insights. He treated her like a valuable human being. He expressed his conviction that people could worship God and please God whatever their geographical, social or religious location and orientation. And then, when she was fully engaged, he showed her that he knew the worst about her life—and he still treated her with dignity and respect. He knew she had been married five times and was now living with a man out of wedlock. Here is Jesus listening to the Holy Spirit and ministering to a wounded heart.

Sue had been meeting with Jason to do Bible study for five months. Jason had been polite, but nothing really seemed to get through to his heart. Sue wasn't even sure why he had agreed to meet with her; she thought he was just lonely (and she was attractive!). Then one day his broken-trust story came out. His dad had died of cancer a year before. Jason had prayed to God, as he understood God, for six months straight, every single day, asking God to heal his dad. His dad had still died. At that point, Jason shut down and his feelings froze. Where was God when his dad died? Why was God so powerless in the face of his personal suffering?

Sue challenged Jason. She asked him if he wanted to live like this, so shut down in his emotions toward people and toward God. Jason looked at Sue, with the pain beginning to seep through his eyes, and told her no, he didn't want to live so shut down. Sue asked if she could pray for his closed-off heart, and he invited her to do that.

As she prayed, she could see his shoulders relax and knew that his heart was beginning to melt. She started by expressing her own questions and doubts about God in the face of her own suffering, and she cried out to God about Jason's suffering. Then she waited on the Holy Spirit to lead her. She felt nudged to pray for healing and for community for Jason, and for a tangible taste of God's presence. Within a few weeks, Jason had come home to God and had begun again to open his heart to others in community.

Like Sue, my antennas are always up, looking for broken trust. I begin by asking for help, expressing my doubts and listening to my friends. You can too. When we discover places of past hurt and broken trust, we can minister to wounded hearts. And there we experience the greatest adventure of having meaningful conversations with spiritual friends on the journey.

After a conference on healing, I was flying home in a plane. I felt nudged by God to talk to the woman next to me. I asked her if she lived in Chicago, where the plane was headed. She told me she did live there and then asked where I was coming from. I told her that I had been at a conference on healing, that God had healed people physically, and that I had received emotional healing in regard to issues in my relationship with my family. She was intrigued, asked questions, then started opening up about her life. She was Jewish and had grown up distrusting Christians, but like me, she had had troubled relationships with family. For her it was with her dad. She felt she needed healing. She wanted to know if Jesus could bring that.

I asked her if I could pray for her. We had a powerful and tender time of prayer, and this woman who had been taught to distrust Jesus expressed a desire to explore and experience Jesus. She was making a major turn toward Christ in her spiritual journey, because she had experienced the presence of God to heal her at her point of pain and broken trust.

Here is the new image of evangelism as conversations on the journey. And here is the new image of us as travel guides who have crossed the terrain of doubts, questions and hurts and received help from the Healer of the brokenhearted.

5

THE POWER OF STORY

I will never forget Abner's story.

Abner, a young professional in Los Angeles, had a Christian friend who was part of a local church for twentysomething people. This church sponsored an outreach event called The Edge. The Edge was an event designed for skeptics, and these edgy meetings were not designed to call people to conversion but only to get them ignited or reignited to pursue the spiritual side of life. Jesus was talked about, but in very noncliché ways. For instance, one meeting was based on the adult cartoon *South Park* and was titled "Jesus vs. the Easter Bunny." Another meeting, on the theme of authenticity, was based on the movie *Face Off.*

Abner's Christian friend invited him to check that meeting out. Abner wasn't interested in Christianity, but he had really liked *Face Off!* So he came.

Later Abner recalled his response. He was very upset. He had written off Christian faith a long time before, but the people he heard that night were not like any Christians he had met. They talked very honestly about struggles and failures. They admitted they didn't have it all together, not just before they "got spiritual"— they still didn't. Doug, the speaker, told of his experiences with marijuana and marijuana look-alikes. He had tried to eat nutmeg once, having heard that it gave a similar high experience. In the midst of the laughter, Doug then challenged those present, re- minding them that neither nutmeg nor marijuana ever really delivered on what they seemed to promise. He also challenged people to pursue the spiritual part of life not through getting high but through opening their hearts to the possibility of God.

Abner was ticked because he was a well-known stoner and drinker. He was rarely completely sober. And he felt like Doug had been reading his mind or at least his mail. He disagreed with Doug, but Abner couldn't ignore the powerful way Doug's story connected to his own life story.

So he asked to get together with Doug. At their meeting, Abner decided he would give God three weeks. And if God didn't show up in three weeks, Abner was done with God. Doug just smiled and nodded.

The next day Abner got high again. He felt like a real hypocrite: he knew that if he kept getting high and drunk, he would not really be giving God a chance. That night he saw where his life was headed. God gave him a vision of what his life would look like without God. In his mind's eye he saw himself older, a forty-year-old divorced alcoholic in despair, sitting and crying on a curb. And he knew this vision wasn't the weed either!

So that night he stopped drinking and smoking, and he hasn't done either since. That night he felt Jesus' presence, and he knew that in that presence he could stop getting drunk and high. During the next three days he continued to sense Jesus' presence, and it freaked him out. *So this is what it feels like to feel God,* he thought.

That weekend, at a party with his friends, he took out his bong (his marijuana water pipe, for you nonstoners out there), and his friends got ready to get high with him. But Abner took the bong, lit it on fire and burned it to ashes. His friends were shocked. "What are you doing? Are you out of your mind?"

Abner responded, "I'm getting rid of what I love the most. I'm not going to do this anymore. My life is going down the drain. I have to trust God."

His friends were blown away. So was Abner's old way of life. He had committed himself to building his identity around a new center, Jesus. He was going to trust Jesus for his security and sense of well-being and no longer look to alcohol and pot.

Over the next months, he joined the church and attended a weekend conference. How strange to be hanging out with all these "crazy Christians"—and to be one of them! Today, just a few years later, he works in ministry with a campus group, reaching out to students struggling just as he was.

Stories are so powerful. Learning to tell our own story, as Abner learned to tell his, is one of the most important steps we take as a Christian. It is not only important for our witness. It is also a crucial step in our self-understanding as a Christian. In many ways, we are the story we tell about ourselves. The art of telling our own story is also the act of discovering and declaring our identity, and of finding the meaning in our lives.

WHY ARE STORIES SO POWERFUL?

My friend Lon Allison believes stories to be the only containers big enough to carry truth, because stories convey not just the facts but also the feelings and nuances of truth. Stories are a bigger and better container for the whole of the truth than propositions, concepts and dogmas. Propositions are wonderful when filled out by story, but abstract and skeletal when divorced from story.

As Eugene Peterson puts it:

The reason that story is so basic to us is that life itself has a

narrative shape—a beginning and an end, plot and characters, conflict and resolution. Life isn't an accumulation of
abstractions such as love and truth, sin and salvation, atone-
ment and holiness; life is the realization of details that all
connect organically, personally, specifically: names and fin-
gerprints, street numbers and local weather, lamb for supper
and a flat tire in the rain. God reveals himself to us not in a
metaphysical formulation or a cosmic fireworks display but in
the kind of stories that we use to tell our children who they
are and how to grow up as human beings. . . . Somewhere
along the way, most of us pick up bad habits of extracting
from the Bible what we pretentiously call "spiritual princi-
ples" or "moral guidelines," or "theological truths," and then
corseting ourselves in them in order to force a godly shape on
our lives.

Jesus taught truth by telling stories, and his stories still reverber-
ate in our souls centuries later: the prodigal son, the sower, the par-
ables of the kingdom. Jesus knew how to lodge truth not just in our
heads but also deeply in our hearts and imaginations. Only stories
can speak to all those levels of us.

In addition, people today tend to distrust logic and truth when it
is expressed propositionally and dogmatically. But when our truth is
enfleshed in the stories of our lives, people are interested. We are a
storytelling culture, in part due to the all-pervasive effect of the me-
dia. Movies and books tell the stories through which we carry on our
cultural discourse about truth and values. Our culture's theologians
are our storytellers. As Willie Jennings at Duke University com-
mented in a recent gathering, "If you want to capture the moral and
spiritual imagination, you invite in the poets and musicians."

And Sarah Hinckley expresses the cry of her media-influenced generation:

> We have every little inconsequential thing, Nintendo 64s and homepages and cell phones, but not one important thing to believe in. What do you have left that will persuade us? One thing: the story. We are story people. We know narratives, not ideas. Our surrogate parents were the TV and the VCR, and we can spew out entertainment trivia at the drop of a hat. . . . You're wondering why we're so self-destructive, but we're looking for the one story with staying power, the destruction and redemption of our own lives. That's to your advantage: You Christians have the best redemption story on the market.

When the metanarratives or Grand Stories die, as they have in our culture, people will be recaptured only by the power of compelling and satisfying stories. Their way back to Christian faith will not first be through logic and proposition and dogma. Their way back will be through the renewal of the Story.

In the past, we thought that worldview was best expressed by answering certain basic questions. What is God like? Who are we? What is our dilemma? How can it be solved? We believed that if we could logically present compelling answers to the basic worldview questions, we could convince people that our worldview was more compelling and coherent than others.

Today we are realizing that answering those basic questions is only one dimension of expressing our worldview compellingly and cogently. As N. T. Wright points out, a worldview consists not just of answers to important questions. Worldviews can be understood best by looking at four dimensions or levels:

1. A Grand Story that founds and frames the worldview. The Christian Grand Story is the story of God's relentless love affair with his people and with all people. The Scriptures as a whole tell the Grand Story of the historical events of God's passionate pursuit of humanity across the ages, cultures and times.

2. Answers to the key worldview questions:
   - Who are we?
   - Where are we?
   - What is the problem?
   - What is the solution?

3. Symbols, both artifacts and cultural events, that give shape and meaning to the worldview. Baptism, Communion, Christmas, Easter, Lent, Pentecost and weekly worship are just a few of these identity-shaping symbols and events.

4. Praxis as the mode of being in the world, the way of life, that the worldview gives rise to. Jesus with his love and justice, walking in the way of the cross and by the power of the Spirit, gives us the pattern of our lives in the world.

People today understand that "story" is a more fundamental category than "proposition," though both are needed. Sometimes Christians' focus on dogma instead of story has resulted in divorcing our truth from the story that gives our truth its meaning, plausibility and power. We must recover our own stories, and God's Big Story, and connect them to the stories of people we love and are reaching out to. Our story. God's story. Their story. The battle for worldview is a battle that takes place first and foremost at the level of the fundamental stories we tell about ourselves and about our faith and about our God.

Where do we start as we reach out to others? We start by learning to tell our own stories. That's what people will connect with first.

WHAT'S THE STORY?

Despite the power of story, we struggle to find meaningful ways and meaningful opportunities to tell others the most important stories about our spiritual journey. Why is it so challenging? The reason is simple: we do not know how to tell our stories in ways that are deeply meaningful and compelling for others, or even for ourselves. Our script for telling our spiritual stories often gets in the way.

One well-meaning leader, after playing a videotape of Abner's story, told at the beginning of this chapter, took most of the power and freshness out of the story by reinterpreting it. We had gotten Abner on tape telling his story while it was fresh. The leader used this video testimony both to encourage people and to critique Abner's mistakes in the telling of his story. For example, he couldn't accept Abner's challenge for God to show up in three weeks. In his mind, that was manipulative. And Abner hadn't said enough about the cross, sin, forgiveness and God's judgment. Was Abner really saved? Abner at least hadn't been taught to tell his story the right way, or else he would have told it better!

For my part, I am thankful that we got Abner on tape before he learned the "right way" to tell his story. Sometimes our "testimony" script gets in the way of telling our real and authentic story. Often new Christians are instructed to edit or change their story in order to fit a script that would properly convey the doctrines that we want the story to communicate. We want people to communicate that they have a sin problem ("my life was messed up before Christ"), that they accepted Jesus' death on the cross to pay for their sin ("I found Jesus as my forgiver and Lord"), and that now their life is much better ("receiving forgiveness and committing to the lordship of Christ has now fixed my life"). This script is a good one, but it's not the only one. It doesn't help many of us to tell our story in a compelling, deeply meaningful way. Doctrine drives the script, and so the story feels contrived. Constrained by this script, we may have trouble even wanting to tell our story.

If you grew up in the church, it's probably even worse for you. You may feel your conversion story is irrelevant to people who didn't grow up in the church. What's more, if you met Christ early in life, your conversion story may feel boring—maybe it *is* a bit boring! I have heard people try to make coming to Christ when they were nine years old interesting. One person I heard put it this way: "I went to church, but I didn't have a relationship with God. I realized I had a sin problem. I struggled with lying to my parents and rebelling against them. Then I met Jesus and received his forgiveness. I felt different, and my parents noticed the change." I don't care how you slice it—that testimony will just never be gripping for the typical skeptic far from God, or even for the person who is telling the story. The dogma drives the story, and it just doesn't feel like an important story.

A friend of mine who grew up in the church went forward every time anyone gave an altar call. Near as he can tell, he "got saved" sixteen times. Which conversion story should he tell?

My friend Kris once attended an evangelism training day. During one of the sessions, people were taught to recount their conversion story. First they were to write it down, then they were to tell it to the group. For some reason, the leader of the training thought it would be motivating and helpful to people to get a grade for their story.

Kris grew up in the church and doesn't have a very dramatic conversion story (though she has some very dramatic "sanctification stories"!), so she wasn't sure what to write. She did her best, wrote down a few thoughts, and then presented them rather self-consciously to the group. The leader gave her a C- on her conversion story!

Needless to say, this experience was not helpful for Kris; it didn't increase her confidence and faith for witness. Her experience is certainly extreme, but it is quite common for Christians, after they tell their scripted conversion story, to lack confidence and motivation to share it with others.

So how do we get beyond a script that doesn't work well for us? How do we generate interest by telling our story when our story may seem boring, confusing or flat?

I suggest that we learn to tell *transformation stories* and move away from being solely focused on our conversion story. Our conversion story is still very important, but only for people who are near the conversion point themselves. Mostly, learning to recount experiences of God's reality and impact is what will help us and others most.

Abner's story is certainly a conversion story, and it is dramatic. Many of us would pay big bucks to have an awesome conversion story like Abner's to tell, though we may not want to go through what he did before he converted! But Abner's story is also a transformation story, and all of us, if we know Jesus, have at least one compelling transformation story to tell. That story may not be about the first time we said a prayer or confessed our sin. We may need to think about other times when God was most real and challenging to us.

Let's look at an example in Scripture of someone who is transformed and then has a story to tell. Let's see what we can learn about telling good transformation stories through this man's example.

AN ENCOUNTER WITH JESUS

In John 9, a blind man encounters Jesus and experiences transformation. He has to turn around and tell his transformation tale immediately and under immense pressure.

Jesus and his followers encounter a blind man on the side of the road. Jesus' followers use the moment as an opportunity to begin a good theological debate about suffering. Whose fault was the blindness? Was it a consequence of this man's sin? But since he had been blind from birth, how could he have sinned? So was it his parents who had sinned? In Jesus' day, this was a good philosophical question. But Jesus didn't take the bait and get into a theological debate. He fought against evil rather than arguing about evil. For many people today, philosophical answers to the problem of evil are much less compelling than the power to heal and to love in the face of evil. Apparently that was true in Jesus' day too!

For Jesus here, the crucial issue is not finding fault and explaining suffering. The crucial issue is healing and transforming sufferers. So Jesus spits on the ground, makes mud, spreads it on the blind man's eyes and sends him to wash it off at a nearby pool. When the man washes off the mud, he can see. What an odd way to heal! What was Jesus doing?

To understand the meaning of the miracle, you need to know the Old Testament background. A similar sort of healing happened through the prophet Elisha around 900 B.C. in Israel. A man named Naaman came to Israel to be healed of leprosy. Elisha promised to heal him so that it would be clear that there was still a prophet in Israel. Elisha sent Naaman to wash himself in the Jordan River, and Naaman emerged clean and free from leprosy. In the John 9 story, this blind man also washes himself in a pool and becomes clean, and in this case able to see.

The transformations in the lives of the leprous man in the Old Testament and the blind man in our story were both powerful. But the miracles also revealed the special identity of Elisha as the prophet in Israel, and in our story the special identity of Jesus as a prophet and the light of the world.

Since the healing of the blind man is understood as a sign of Jesus' identity, the man comes under a lot of pressure to explain away what has happened. The religious leaders hate Jesus' claims about himself and his identity. So they try to get the formerly blind man first to deny who he was, then to deny that it was Jesus who had healed him, and finally to testify that Jesus did it because he was a terrible sinner.

The man just keeps telling his transformation story: "I was blind, but now I see." He doesn't have any particular script (though some people have turned his story into a script and formula!). He just tells how he encountered Jesus, what Jesus did, how he responded and what happened to him as a result. The leaders end up kicking the blind man out of the synagogue because he won't turn against Jesus.

Later Jesus finds the formerly blind man and finishes the work of transformation. The end result: this blind man is the first recorded person to worship Jesus. He sees before anyone else who Jesus really is. And the people who ought to have seen, the church types, remain blind to the transforming presence and reality of God. I wonder if that ever happens today . . .

I want to highlight a few things that can help us tell our spiritual and transformational stories:

1. The issue for the man was blindness, not sin. His story, rather than focusing on how sinful he was, kept on being a story

about how he wasn't as sinful or as much to blame as everyone else assumed. We often think that if we haven't talked about sin, we haven't evangelized. Not true. This man was blind and then he was healed, both physically and spiritually. Notice who keeps bringing up the man's sin. Not Jesus. Not the man. First the followers of Jesus and then the religious leaders. It was the religious types who kept obsessing about the man's sin!

Just to avoid misunderstanding here, let me assure you we will get to sin! I'm not arguing for leaving that out—especially today when our culture pushes us to leave it out. My point is, we tend to assume we have to focus on sin to really be evangelizing, and that's not true, especially when it comes to telling our transformation stories. Sin and guilt may or may not have been an important part of our conscious experience during times of transformation. We tell what happened and what we experienced, not what we think should have happened!

2. The formerly blind man's story, until he met Jesus again, wasn't theologically very sophisticated. He didn't have a theology, he had an experience. He recounted the experience. Only later, as people pushed him and then he met Jesus and was told more, did the theological interpretation become part of the transformation story. We need to learn to tell our stories of spiritual and transformational experiences without interference of a theological script and interpretation. An interpretation layer comes as the story itself intrigues people and they want to know how we interpret what happened to us. Notice, the religious people push the man by saying that Jesus is a sinner. At first the man simply says, "I can't comment on that. What I know is that I was blind and now I see."

Too often our excessive dependence on theological inter-pretations robs our story of its freshness and resonance for others. Also, the tendency to preemptively provide our theo-logical interpretation, rather than beginning with just our spiritual and transformational experience, often makes us feel disconnected from our own story. We make it fit the for-mat we think it should have, and it loses its power as an au-thentic personal story.

3. When the blind man did get to the theological interpretation, it flowed naturally from his story and was not an imposition on it. Here's his basic plot: "I was healed. Jesus did it. Only proph-ets do that sort of thing. Jesus must be a prophet. You all are obsessed by him. Do you want to be his disciples too?"

4. The end result for the man born blind is that he was willing to lose solidarity with his parents, approval from his "church" and acceptance from his friends. His identity was now ori-ented toward Jesus. His security rested in Jesus. And his loyalty was toward Jesus. Here is true transformation on every level of his being.

WHAT'S YOUR STORY?

The man born blind knew his transformation story and told it well in the face of great opposition. Do you have a story to tell? Do you know what it is? Are you ready to tell it?

When in your life was God most real to you? When has your en-counter with Jesus been most influential? When have you most connected to the reality of the spiritual side of life? That's your cru-cial story to learn to share. That's the story that will be most rele-vant for you as a guide for others in the spiritual journey.

If you don't have any evidence that God is real and active and can change lives, you may not have a lot to share with people today, for many tend to be more concerned about God's reality than about God's reasonableness. You may have good reasons for your faith. You may have good historical evidence. But do you have personal, experiential evidence? Do you know, not just from others and not just in your head, but also in your heart and from your own experience, that Jesus is real and following Jesus has rocked your world? If you don't have such evidence, the first step is to get some! You can't share about how God transforms people unless you have experienced it.

I can tell transformation stories from every era of my life, stories related to many struggles I have had. As a result, I have transformation stories to tell people from many different ages, stages and walks of life. If you have a vital, growing relationship with God, you have the same potential. Your transformation stories are the most potent gift you can give to others in their spiritual journey toward God.

In college, my transformation story was related to dating and always needing to have a girlfriend. Girls were at the center of my life, where I put my identity and sense of well-being. You can read this transformation story in the little booklet *Circles of Belonging* (published by InterVarsity Press). That transformation story is also my conversion story.

In my twenties, my transformation story was about my life work. Would I stay an engineer and accrue money and status, or would I go with my heart and do what I felt most gifted to do and what would most contribute to the lives of others? During this time, I learned to hear God's voice personally. So many people pray and want direction at critical decision points, but have no idea that God cares enough about them to speak concretely into their life. My transformation story from this period of my life can encourage them to learn to recognize and listen to God's voice as part of their decision making.

In my thirties, my transformation story was about my marriage. I was a workaholic and centered my identity in my work. I was losing the relationships that were most important. My wife, MaryKay, couldn't figure out why I even wanted to be married. She was alone in a new city taking care of a two-year-old, lonely and upset that her husband's priorities had gotten so screwed up. I nearly crashed and burned at that point and had to seek healing for the fundamental issues and hurts that were erupting. During that period, God probably became more real to me than ever before. My drivenness and neediness were at their highest pitch. That made me a prime candidate for God's healing power and for changing the locus of my identity. My marriage transformation story is the greatest gift I can give to others who are struggling the way I did.

In every stage of life, and through many different experiences, you have a story to tell. If you don't have any transformation story to share, maybe you aren't really a Christ follower yet. You may be running on the faith of your parents or the force of your church background. When I teach people the journey-guide model of witness, there are often people in the group who think they are believers but don't have much evidence of God's reality in their life. They have no transformation story to tell. I challenge them to seek God's transforming reality for themselves. Some of them become Christ followers at that point! Then they have something to share with others. More important, they have truly begun the spiritual adventure of following Jesus for themselves.

CONNECTING OUR STORIES TO OTHERS

In addition to having a transformation story and being able to tell it, we need to learn the skill of connecting our story to the needs and stories of other people. They will be interested in our story, but only if they think it will be relevant to their life and story. But how do we make that connection?

The connecting point is our shared humanity, our common struggles and sufferings, needs and longings. So we ask God for discernment and opportunity to share out of that shared humanity. Where do you identify with your friend? How can you open up your needs and struggles in ways that welcome your friend's opening her own door for vulnerability?

Then, as you have found common struggles and sufferings, needs and longings, you can speak of how your spiritual experiences and connection to God have helped you in the midst of your struggles. Keep your statements brief—that makes them intriguing. Don't look for ways that you are stronger, better or more successful than your friend. Look for the similar struggles and hurts. And then talk from your heart about the difference closeness to God has made.

Less is better. Make a few heartfelt and vulnerable comments, and then let your friends reveal to you how deep their trust and how great their interest is. Ask them if they relate to what you have said. If your friend is interested, he will let you know and invite you to say more. When trust is there and vulnerability is real, people love hearing the transformation stories of others. Your friends will love hearing yours, as long as it feels genuine and not cliché, nor agenda driven.

Your struggles, sufferings, needs and longings are the best bridge into the lives of others. And your transformation stories are your greatest personal asset for sharing your faith. If you have any tales of transformation, you can be a great witness to the love and power of God.

6

JESUS OUTSIDE THE BOX

Mark is a young professional who works at Lucent Technologies, a local company. Ron also works at Lucent. Besides being one of the nicest guys Mark has ever met, Ron is also Mark's friend who loses wallets and has an ulcer, and for whom Mark often finds himself praying (kind of like Sam at Einstein Bagels for me!).

One day Mark prayed for Ron, asking God for the next step in relationship and witness. Later, as Mark was filling up his chocolate macadamia-nut coffee at the company coffee urn, Ron wandered by. Earlier that week Mark had told Ron that he had been to a conference on healing and was amazed at how God had powerfully healed some very hurting people. Now Ron, clearly responding to the earlier spiritual conversation, suddenly blurted out a question Mark wasn't expecting. Ron expressed his conviction—a common one in our culture—that it doesn't really matter what people believe; as long as they find what works for them, that is what's important. Then he turned to Mark and asked with an edge in his voice, "You're not one of those people that believe there's only one way, are you?"

What do you say to that one? Here Mark had been innocently getting his coffee and thinking about his work for the day, and suddenly he was confronted by one of the toughest questions (accusations?) committed believers of any faith face. And Mark could tell by Ron's voice that if he admitted he was one of *those people*, Ron wouldn't be talking to Mark about Christian faith again. Ron might as well have been asking, "You aren't one of those terrorists, are you?" It's not that he would really equate Mark with a terrorist, but in the predominant cultural perception, it is people who believe there is only one way who often appear in the news, judging, rejecting and sometimes even killing others in the name of their god.

I think Mark handled it well, and I want to recommend his approach. Mark's immediate response was to say, "I'm certainly not one of those people who judge and reject everybody who doesn't believe what I believe. I hate that. I think Jesus would have hated that kind of self-righteous attitude too." At that point, Mark later told me, he could almost hear Ron's sigh of relief. Ron was clearly glad he wasn't talking to one of *those* people.

Mark didn't leave it there, though. He continued, "At the same time, I do believe Jesus is uniquely the way into a relationship with God. And I want to ask you a question along this line. You said before that it doesn't matter what people believe, as long as it works for them. But could there be good spiritualities and bad spiritualities, good beliefs and bad beliefs?"

Ron wasn't sure what Mark meant. So Mark went a little further, "I think some spiritualities are fairly self-centered. They don't really lead us out of ourselves and into loving others or God. I think those kinds of spiritualities, though common, are not good spiritualities. I think Jesus confronted self-absorbed spirituality. If our spirituality doesn't connect us to something much bigger than ourselves and doesn't influence us toward becoming other centered, Jesus would probably confront it. Most of the spirituality that fills our culture is self-centered. People today are spiritually interested, but they want spiritual experience and spiritual reality on their own terms. They want spirituality, but they don't want to have to change. Jesus confronts and rejects that type of spirituality. He loves people enough not to leave them with such self-centered beliefs. What do you think?"

Ron got very quiet and told Mark he would have to think about it. Then he asked Mark to pray that he could stop drinking so much. It wasn't that he thought drinking was wrong, only that he was afraid he might have a problem.

That day Mark and Ron made a lot of progress together on the spiritual journey! In fact, Mark helped Ron move a step toward commitment to the uniqueness of Jesus, even though he didn't take the issue head on then and there.

I do believe Jesus meant what he said when he said that there is no way to the Father but through Jesus. Jesus is uniquely the way to a relationship with God the Father. But when I answer people who ask me questions like Ron's, I pay attention to their stereotypes and misunderstandings. And, like Mark, I will not play into those misunderstandings and stereotypes.

Jesus did the same thing often. When people asked him questions that were intended to trap him, he answered on his own terms and not on theirs. Often he confronted them, but he did not play into their stereotypes. We face the same challenge today. Breaking people's stereotypes in order to enter into genuine and challenging spiritual conversations is especially important when it comes to speaking about Jesus with contemporary seekers and skeptics.

CLICHÉ JESUS

Sooner or later, whatever model of witness you pursue, the crucial issue will always be Jesus. But people today think they know about Jesus; they don't want to talk about Jesus with church people who, they think, are trying to convert them. Seekers and skeptics also have the impression that church people talk about Jesus in cliché and uninteresting ways.

Seekers and skeptics expect this kind of language from church people:

- I asked Jesus into my heart.
- Are you saved (or born again)?
- Jesus loves you.
- I found it. Have you?
- Jesus can make your life so much better. He can fulfill you.
- Whatever the question, Jesus is the answer!

Seekers and skeptics often expect church people to talk about a washed-out, domesticated Jesus, someone who helps you control life, manage your image and keep you from letting go and having fun.

As one of my InterVarsity associates likes to say, Jesus is more like Warhead candy than like tofu. Let me tell you what I mean.

I love Japanese food, and when I go to a Japanese restaurant, I always ask for miso soup. A bowl of miso soup generally includes several chunks of floating tofu. Tofu almost never provokes a strong response. It's mild, bland, gelatinous. It enhances (or detracts from, depending on how you respond to its consistency) whatever else you are eating with it. But tofu will never make or break a meal. It's always in the background, nice but not very noticeable.

Warhead candy is very different. It sneaks up on you. At first you think you are just sucking on a nice jawbreaker or hard candy. Then, unexpectedly, it explodes in your mouth with flavor and sourness.

Jesus is more like Warhead candy. He may appear innocuous at first, but nothing will ever be the same in life once you have really encountered Jesus.

What are our boxes around Jesus that make him a tame, cliché Jesus? For many, the following list would look familiar.

- Jesus is Swedish and blue-eyed, especially if you're from a white ethnic background. After all, that's what his picture shows in many European-origin churches.

- Jesus is always nice. He always looks at you with those kind eyes and never has a harsh word to say to anyone. And of course Jesus would never swear or shout. He's much too holy for that!

- Jesus' favorite hobby is cuddling sheep. In the pictures we saw of him when we were young, he's always holding sheep or kids.

- Jesus is mystical, melancholy and otherworldly. We don't picture him at parties or hanging out at a ballgame.

- Jesus hates conflict. He is always dialing down situations, answering critics meekly, turning the other cheek.

In many ways we follow an easy-listening Jesus, tame and soothing, into religion and image and control. He is a jack-in-the-box Jesus. You never know when he will pop out; it might happen at any moment. But you always know what he will look like: artificial and cliché. The easy-listening, all-purpose solution to all the problems of life.

OUTSIDE-THE-BOX JESUS

When we engage with Scripture, though, we find that Jesus is anything but bland. He is a confusing combination of opposites, more like Warhead candy.

Jesus elicits a fierce love-hate relationship with everything and everybody he meets. It's very surprising to see who and what he loved and who and what loved or hated him.

He hung out with sinners, sick people, lepers, prostitutes, drunkards, blue-collar types. If you felt second class, like a failure, not a religious person, alienated by church and by spiritual-type people, then Jesus loved hanging out with you, and you loved hanging out with Jesus.

In contrast, Jesus didn't much like hanging out with the religious leaders and in the religious institutions of his day. He felt they were more into money and their own image and status than into compassion and people and God. One time Jesus visited the temple, the most important religious institution of his day, he started turning over tables, driving out animals and waving a whip around at people. Not much like tofu. He was very angry that the religious institutions of his day were not helping poor folks, women and people of other cultures find God (see Mark 11).

Have you ever felt alienated from religious institutions or had trouble connecting or relating to them? Have you ever struggled with their apparent focus on money, image and control? Maybe you are more in tune with Jesus than you ever realized.

Jesus was an odd combination of opposites in another way too. He was incredibly human, incredibly approachable. And yet he was also disturbingly different.

He was human in his enjoyment of life. He partied, he ate a lot, he hung out with friends, and he went off for rest and relaxation. His first miracle was to turn water into wine and make a good party great (see John 2)! He was also human in his loneliness and pain. He wept at death, he got hungry and tired and tempted, he felt lonely and humiliated, he needed his friends; he asked God to change his circumstances, experienced unanswered prayer and then died very painfully.

Yet he was strangely different too. He healed people, forgave sins, chose to identify with the worst kind of people. When he experienced the death of a friend, he wept, just as you and I would. But then he did something very unusual: he raised his friend from the dead. John 11 tells that story. Jesus himself also died the most painful and humiliating death. And like Jesus, we will all die someday. But Jesus didn't stay dead.

Another confusing tension Jesus held together was his intensely arrogant humility. He was humble and other centered. He washed the feet of his followers—a task that was supposed to be left to slaves and servants. He used his power to serve and love and not to dominate. He cared for people when nobody else did. But he was alarmingly arrogant too. He said, "I am the way the truth and the life; no one comes to the Father but by me." When a blind man worshiped him, and when a doubting man fell at his feet and called him "my Lord and my God," he accepted their worship. When he was facing a death sentence, he told Pontius Pilate, the ruler in Jerusalem, that Pilate had no real power over him. Not a way to win friends and influence people.

Tofu or Warhead candy? Have you ever encountered the real Jesus? Have you ever looked with fresh eyes past the Jesus stereotypes? It's an adventure you will never forget, and it will probably change your life, whether you are a skeptic or have been a Jesus follower for years.

TOUGH QUESTIONS

A couple of chapters back, I challenged you to consider that the breach in trust that seekers and skeptics often have toward God, Christians and the church is not an obstacle to spiritual conversation but an opportunity, if you start by identifying with their mistrust. Similarly, in this chapter I want to challenge you to consider the toughest questions we face from seekers and skeptics as opportunities for significant spiritual conversation and engagement.

The questions I most often hear include the following:

1. How can you believe that Jesus is the only way and that you're right and everybody else is wrong? That is so narrow.

2. How can you judge the lifestyle and identity of other people—for instance, gay and lesbian people? That is so judgmental.

3. Where was God when I or those I love suffered? How do you know God is real?

In my book *Evangelism Outside the Box,* I suggested that there are questions behind these questions that are even more fundamental and must be addressed first. Some of these more fundamental questions are as follows:

1. *Questions of power and motive.* To many people today, we're just another tribe or interest group, using our logic to gain power.

2. *Questions of identity.* How can you Christians think you can tell other people who they are? Each person has to create her own meaning and identity.

3. *Questions of trust.* Why should I trust you? Look at what believers have done: Racism. Sexism. Homophobia. The Crusades. Religious wars. You are constantly drawing lines of exclusion.

4. *Questions of community.* Isn't the way you see the world completely dependent on your community and place of birth?

Whenever Jesus faced the tough questions in his day, he responded brilliantly, in ways that led to intense, illuminating moments of decision for the people with whom he was talking. Jesus chose those moments to become confrontational, but in unexpected ways. He didn't fit the stereotypes or go by the rules of his questioner. He often addressed the questions behind the questions first. In so doing, he broke out of the questioners' stereotypes and rules. And then Jesus confronted people's false ways of understanding God and spirituality. One such encounter was with a man named Nicodemus (John 3).

JESUS CONFRONTS RELIGIOUS ELITISM

Nicodemus approaches Jesus by night, so as not to be seen. We don't know the whole reason Nicodemus felt he had to sneak around, but John gives us some clues. Just before Nicodemus visits Jesus, John tells us the story of Jesus' visit to the temple. The temple was the most important religious institution of Jesus' day and culture. You can often discern the spirit of an age or a nation by looking at the most culturally affirmed institutions, including the most culturally affirmed religious institutions.

At the temple, Jesus made a whip out of cords and chased out sheep and cattle. Notice, here is one time when Jesus didn't cuddle sheep but drove them with a whip. Then he overturned all the commercial booths and tables. Finally, he yelled at the sellers, telling them to get out. They had turned the area where common people and people of other cultures were to find God in prayer into a noisy, successful commercial venture. Jesus was Angry with a capital *A*! Then Jesus made a cryptic comment about replacing the temple with his own body—a comment that horrified the religious leaders and completely bewildered his followers. They didn't understand the comment until after his death and its aftermath.

Nicodemus, a member of the ruling council that was often in the temple, visited Jesus after this tempestuous incident. No wonder he came at night. His friends on the ruling council were probably cursing Jesus, not calling on him with their spiritual questions.

Nicodemus compliments Jesus on his miracles and acknowledges that Jesus must be a rabbi from God to perform such amazing feats. Jesus responds by telling Nicodemus that all Nicodemus's religious learning counts for very little. Nicodemus is a teacher of Israel, he points out, and yet doesn't know the first thing about spiritual reality. He basically tells Nicodemus he must give up his pride in his learning and his spiritual achievements and that he must start over. Eyes of "flesh," eyes that see things only according to the spirit of the world and of the age, are blind. Only eyes enlightened by God's Spirit can see things from God's viewpoint.

Jesus breaks Nicodemus's stereotypes of what a religious leader should say, and he changes the rules. Nicodemus has come to put Jesus on trial, but Jesus turns the tables. He does so by confronting the spirit of his age, at least as it expressed itself in the Israel of that day.

The spirit of Jesus' age in that nation was the spirit of religious elitism. People believed that those who kept themselves "pure" and worshiped God in the right way and the right place were better than other people, acceptable to God. Jesus confronted this narrow, judgmental, exclusive type of spirituality. Religious types didn't like Jesus much. He challenged their whole way of looking at the world, telling them they needed to become like children, start over, become inclusive, be born of the Spirit. But he got their attention, and he reframed the whole conversation. When Jesus talked about being born again, it was not a slogan or cliché. It was a whole new way of saying that the least and the lost were now humble enough to turn to God and the spiritually proud were being excluded.

CONFRONTING SPIRITUAL CONSUMERISM

The spirit of religious elitism is alive and well today, and we need to confront it when we face it, in ourselves and in others. But I would suggest that one of the predominant spirits of our age, at least in the West, is *spiritual consumerism.*

People today love spirituality, but they want to make up their own version. For twenty-first-century people, spirituality is like a smorgasbord. They want to pick from the buffet line of spiritual ideas whatever resonates for them. If you choose to become a Christ follower, that's fine—whatever floats your boat. But don't expect them to do the same. What's true for you may not be true for them.

This spirit of spiritual consumerism is not just obvious in the broader culture. It is often just as prevalent in the church. You can find it in liberal churches whose spiritual temperament is redolent of New Age thinking. But you can find it in conservative churches too. People hop from church to church, looking at each church from the viewpoint of a spiritual consumer, and don't even question this basic approach.

At some point we have to challenge people and the spirit of our age. It is a spirituality-of-me generation and world. We have to confront this me-centered spirituality. But we struggle to do so, because we know people will be offended.

The good news about Jesus is fundamentally different from the good news of spiritual consumerism! We have to confront apathy and the sense that there is really nothing at stake.

Christian faith tells us that we are not God. That may not sound like good news, but it is! People would create a very messed-up place if we were God. In the movie *Bruce Almighty,* Bruce finds a way to answer every prayer. The world descends into the chaos of everybody getting what they want. For instance, everybody who buys a ticket and prays wins the lottery. At first people are overjoyed, but then they find out that with so many people winning, everybody gets about $1.50. Riots ensue.

We are morally accountable and will stand before God someday and be judged. That may sound like bad news. But it's *good* news! If anything goes, if people's actions didn't really matter, than justice would never be done and the world would never get well. It's good news that we're accountable.

If you and I decide to do whatever we want to do, we'll be judged. That may be bad news for individuals, but it's good news for a world in desperate need of justice and accountability.

God is the Absolute and therefore the judge of what it means to be human. That's not bad news, that's good news—there's a way out of the chaos and confusion.

Although spiritual consumerism seems like a great deal, at the end of the day it leads to self-absorption, self-centeredness, self-futility, ultimately death at the core of our being. The Bible names that self-centeredness as sin, and the end result of it is the hell of self alone, without God and without hope.

Me-centered spirituality is ultimately futile and damnable. It is futile and damnable whether we find it in the broader culture or find it in the church.

How do we challenge me-centered spirituality?

First we must confront it in ourselves. Only the transformation of our own lives will allow us to authentically challenge others. Do you hop from community to community? Have you been infected by the disease of spiritual consumerism? Have you been part of church splits? Or are you part of a church that teaches a universalistic and morally vague spirituality? Do you focus only on the parts of Jesus that are comfortable for you? The first step is to see, admit and turn from the ways spiritual consumerism has shaped our own hearts and habits.

I have had to face my own tendencies toward me-centered spirituality in some of the healing ministries I have led and been part of. Sometimes others have had to confront me. I have found myself wanting dramatic experiences of "feeling God" to happen over and over again. At other times, I have had to challenge people who came to me for prayer, asking for God to heal them and never seeming to get beyond a self-centered focus on their own needs. I have at points had to ask, "Can you for one moment think of something not yourself?" Spiritual consumerism pervades our culture and influences all of us at some level.

Next, we need to see where Jesus confronts spiritual consumerism, and learn from him. Sometimes our "gospel of grace" seems to imply that we can accept Jesus while avoiding change, and it thus becomes a gospel of *cheap* grace. Study and live the Sermon on the Mount for the next few months; let that discipline expose to you the gospel of cheap grace and the currents of spiritual consumerism in our culture, and you will be changed.

Finally, we need to learn skills of loving confrontation. When people tell us, "Whatever floats your boat," we need to have good responses—something like "Sure, but just make sure you're not riding on the *Titanic!* Are there bad, destructive or life-undermining spiritualities? Are there good beliefs and bad beliefs? What's the difference between a good spirituality and a bad spirituality? I see a lot of spirituality out there that doesn't get people out of self-absorption and self-centeredness. If spirituality doesn't get us beyond self-centeredness and self-absorption into a bigger life and a larger perspective, I think, it's a bad spirituality. What do you think?" When we do confront me-centered spirituality, people may not like us. I think of my friend Dave. We all thought Dave had become a Christian. He had "prayed the prayer," was coming to church regularly and had even been baptized. Then we found out what Dave believed about Jesus. He saw Jesus in ways similar to the picture of Jesus in *The Da Vinci Code*. In Dave's view, Jesus was insightful and revolutionary, but he wasn't divine any more than you and I are divine. Jesus expressed the god potential in all of us, but we are still free to live any way we want. When I finally discovered and confronted Dave's views of Jesus, he got very offended and never wanted to talk to me again.

The spiritual consumerism of our age is a powerful spiritual deception, and people will not come out of it easily. As often as not, they will be offended and work hard to hold on to a version of faith that leaves them in charge and able to pick and choose. Of course, in these moments we are merely following in the footsteps of Jesus, who offended a lot of people when he confronted the spirit of his age. I don't mind an offended response when I speak about the uniqueness of Jesus. I just want people to be offended for the right reasons—I don't want to confirm their stereotypes regarding anyone who believes that there is only one way.

People will ask us, "How can you believe Jesus is the only way? How can you be that narrow?" Let's break out of the stereotyped response they expect and first address the trust question that lies behind the stated question. Then we can change the framework of the discussion and put them on the spot. We can say, "I am not one of those people who believe that I am right and everybody else is wrong. I can't stand that kind of arrogance and self-righteousness. I too am a learner, every day. But I do think Jesus is uniquely the path to a relationship with God. And along that line, I have a question for *you*. Do you think it matters what we believe? Do you think the relativists are right and we can believe whatever we want, as long as it works for us?" Then we go from there. May God give us the courage to confront the spirit of spiritual consumerism in our day.

When any tough question is posed to us, we do well to listen for the questions behind the question and then defuse the stereotype, state our conviction and turn the question around. These questions can become important opportunities to take the conversation deeper and the relationship further.

SPEAKING ABOUT JESUS

In our conversations with friends (and acquaintances!) on a spiritual journey, Jesus will surprise people—not by popping up constantly but by looking very different from the expected when he does appear. People are repelled by the cliché Jesus, the one they see in most churches. But they are very attracted to the outside-the-box Jesus and want to encounter him.

At the end of the day, witness is all about Jesus. It's not about you and it's not about me, though Jesus has included our stories in his. It's all about him. So sooner or later, witness will lead us to talk about Jesus with others. But how do we do that? How do we bring Jesus into our conversations? How do we make Jesus the focus? How do we overcome the barriers of people's assumed knowledge and lack of interest?

The crucial skill we need at this point in the conversational dance is to bring up Jesus and speak about him in ways that break the stereotypes and break through the apathy. Our crucial question is: How does Jesus break our stereotypes of Jesus? How do we introduce people to the outside-the-box Jesus, the one who hated religiousness, loved making wine for parties, always stood up for the underdog, and gave the stuck-up and self-righteous hell? How do we learn to talk about that real Jesus?

AN OUTSIDE-THE-BOX SEEKER SMALL GROUP

Many church and parachurch movements have discovered GIGs (groups investigating God), also called seeker small groups, to be a very powerful way for individuals and small groups to speak about Jesus today. All you need to begin a seeker small group is at least one unchurched friend. A seeker small group is a spiritual discussion group for two or more people. If you're interested in learning more about seeker small groups, you will find some great resources pictured in the back of this book.

Let me tell you about one of the most surprising seeker small groups I ever participated in, to show you how they work and to intrigue you with what can happen.

I began one of my first seeker groups because five teens felt sorry for me. I was on a short-term summer missions trip in Ireland one summer. A Christian woman had asked me to speak at a local Catholic charismatic prayer meeting. I was in the town of Thurles, 99 percent Roman Catholic, at a time when Irish small-town Roman Catholicism had not yet been affected much by the renewal associated with Vatican II.

After I gave a short testimony and encouraged people to trust and follow Jesus, Sean exploded out of his seat and confronted me.

"Are you Catholic?" he shot out.

"I was baptized Catholic," I replied, truthfully.

Not satisfied, he continued to grill me. "Do you believe in the Virgin Mary?"

"I believe everything the Bible says about her," I replied. I thought I was being fairly clever. He didn't seem to agree. He got angrier and angrier, until he finally threatened me with words I will never forget: "I think I'm going to throw you out of this window!" We were on the second story.

I had read the stories about the persecution of Paul in the book of Acts. Suddenly those stories were feeling a little more relevant.

Sean proceeded to pick me up (he was about six feet three inches and quite stocky) and carry me about three feet; then he paused, confronted by five compassionate teens.

They spoke up: "Sean, put him down. You don't want to kill the guy, do you? You don't want to go to jail, do you?" When they mentioned the killing part, Sean didn't respond, but the jail part seemed to get through. He dropped me flat on the floor and stalked out. Those five Catholic teenagers saved my life that day!

The five young people then apologized. They offered to study the Bible with me; they knew that was what I wanted. Before the incident with Sean, I think only one of them might have joined my seeker small group. But since they all felt sorry for me, all five joined me, and we began to meet that next week.

We studied Jesus' encounter with Peter in chapter 5 of Luke, when Peter falls at Jesus' feet begging for mercy after Jesus helps him and his friends and family catch a boatload of fish. Peter expected Jesus to speak with authority about religious things, but not about fishing. Fishing was Peter's thing. But Jesus wanted to break out of Peter's box and show Peter his power in all of life.

So I asked about how Jesus might be trusted in the different arenas of our own lives. Patrick interrupted me midsentence and began arguing with himself. "I want to trust and follow Jesus . . . But my parents might think I've become a Protestant and reject me . . . But I think Jesus is real, and I think I need him . . . But I will have to change my life . . . But I know Jesus will help me . . . But I am afraid of what it will mean . . ." Patrick went on in this back-and-forth way for about five minutes. Finally he ended his argument with himself, saying, "But I just need to do this." Promptly he got down on his knees and committed himself to Jesus as his forgiver and leader.

The group sat stunned. The other three who had not yet made that commitment to Jesus (one was already a committed follower of Christ) knew their days were numbered. And indeed, within a couple of weeks all of them had entered the kingdom.

To put it mildly, I was surprised by everything that happened in this seeker small group, from the near-death experience, through the unorthodox way to recruit members, through the conversion of all the people who didn't already know and follow Jesus. In some ways this experience was unique. And yet after leading seeker small groups for the past twenty-five years, I am still always surprised, challenged and changed when I begin and lead one. I am always amazed by the profoundly positive reaction people have when they look at Jesus' life, as pictured in the Gospels, up close and personal.

Why are seeker small groups so often so powerful? Because they let the outside-the-box, delightful, disturbing Jesus speak and act for himself. People can't help but be intrigued, surprised and wooed. And that encounter with Jesus in the Scriptures opens the door for us to share the ways Jesus broke open our boxes and rocked our world. *That* Jesus our friends will want to talk about!

7

GREAT NEWS!

How did you encounter the reality and authority of Jesus? What message did you hear? How did you respond?

In my ninth-grade year, I met Dan. He sat next to me in class, a transfer student looking for friends. He had grown up in a Christian home, and in the midst of our various experiments with ESP and Ouija boards, he also invited me to church events. On one of them, a summer week at the beach for high-school students, I encountered a sense of the reality of Jesus and the call to give my life to his leadership. I was also encouraged to trust God for the forgiveness of my sins.

I remember walking on the Ocean City boardwalk until three in the morning, trying to decide if I would commit myself to trusting and following Jesus. I knew it wouldn't be easy, because my parents would be against it. They saw evangelical faith not only as anti-intellectual but also as a conservative drag on the liberal issues of justice and personal liberty that they were very committed to. But I finally decided to go for it.

The next day, my group leader called me over to tell my story to two hundred people he had gathered on the beach and to whom he was preaching, using a microphone and speaker. After I spoke, the group leader invited all of us who had committed our lives to Christ to be baptized in the Atlantic Ocean. Forty of us were baptized that day. It was quite a moment, with the surf pounding and the sun shining red over the turbulent waters.

I flourished for a while in my newfound faith. I remember fasting, and then living on peanut butter and white bread for a couple of weeks. I returned home and confronted my two brothers and several kids in the neighborhood with how crucial it was for them to respond to Christ. I had a hard-hitting style of evangelism, returning often to the theme of hell. I think I got three "conversions" in the next few weeks, but they all had to be done over later by the victims of my evangelistic outburst.

By the time I got to college, I was firmly back in the camp of atheism. I had even become good at arguing people out of faith, demonstrating how full of intellectual holes it was. My girlfriend at the time still hasn't completely recovered. But then I met thoughtful, loving people in a campus fellowship and recommitted my life. Once again, I stayed up until three in the morning battling. This time I had to decide whether to give my relationship with my girlfriend to God. I didn't want to stop doing what we were doing, nor did I want to give up the intimacy we had. But I knew that I had to choose. I chose to follow Jesus. I will never forget that awkward night of visiting my girlfriend, home from Princeton at the time, and breaking off our relationship. Not only was she very upset, but her dad nearly punched me because of how I was hurting his only daughter! That choice kicked off a rich and full time in my life. Over the next several years, I grew by studying the Bible, praying, living out my faith in a fraternity and sharing my faith with those still far from God.

The message I heard was about the loving authority of Jesus, over the world and over my life. In each case I had to respond to Jesus' authority not on my own terms but on his. First I had to make a choice my family might never understand, and later I had to give up a relationship with a person I loved.

What's the message people need to hear and experience if they are to have the opportunity to respond to God? How can we share that message?

THE GOSPEL IN POST-CHRISTIAN CULTURE

In post-Christian culture, people see the gospel as neither good nor news. When they hear the word *gospel,* they think of a style of music or of oldtime tent meetings with tacky sentimental hymns, slick preachers and emotional excess. But seekers and skeptics are not the only people who have problems in their perceptions of the Christian gospel. Believers are struggling today as well. Many believers are not at all sure that the gospel is good or that it's news. It feels old and dogmatic, not fresh and alive. Christians know they should feel waves of gratitude whenever they think about how Christ died for their sins, but somehow the feelings don't come and the message doesn't inspire. And so when an opportunity arises to share the "good news" with another person, Christians are often neither ready nor excited to do so. Many Christians are not even looking for opportunities any longer to communicate the gospel and would be shocked if someone they knew was actually interested in hearing the message about "sin and the cross."

What's gone wrong? How can the freshness and enthusiasm of having great news be restored?

My conviction is that evangelical believers are too familiar with the message and have simplified and codified it to the extent of breeding apathy.

To seekers and skeptics, meanwhile, most of the ideas that we try to communicate in relation to the gospel are foreign. The role and rights of a Creator over the creation, the accountability of humanity to God, the depth and horror of sin and evil, the rightness of the wrath and justice of God, the forgiveness of sins through a horrible Jewish death on a wooden cross two thousand years ago, Jesus' return to life after death, and God's intervention at the end of history to establish God's dominance are all ideas that make very little sense to people nurtured in the liberal, secular, subjective postmodern culture. Where do you even begin? How do you communicate such foreign ideas to people who value experience before explanation and story over dogma?

WHAT IS THE GOOD NEWS?

The good news is as much about the present as it is about what happens after we die. People, Christian and not, perceive the good news as neither good nor news, because it doesn't seem to have much to say that's compelling about the life in the world. Certainly, as one of my friends puts it, "Life is hard; God is here, and heaven is real." But heaven is not just "pie in the sky by and by." Heaven begins in the here and now (what Jesus called the kingdom of heaven).

When Jesus announced the good news of the kingdom, which is the inbreaking and dynamic rule of God to set all things right, he wasn't talking only about what would happen after people died. He was talking about the personal and social transformation that had begun with his coming. The news was good because God was setting all things right. The news was news because the long-awaited moment had finally come, the gun had finally gone off. The most important and newsworthy events in all of history were happening right there in front of people's eyes.

The immediate experiences people had upon hearing this news

were validating: liberation, forgiveness, healing. People were being set free from sin, sickness and spiritual oppression. This experience of transformation demanded an explanation, and Jesus gave one: the rule of God to set all things right had invaded history. You could see it in the eyes of the sick, the hurting, the discouraged and the poor. The spiritual malaise gripping people and the nation was lifting.

Not everyone was happy with this news, or with the herald of it. The religious, who benefited by the way things were, felt threatened. They, with the help of their Gentile rulers, put Jesus to death. And then, *surprise:* the defeat turned out to be the victory. The seed of Jesus' life had fallen into the ground, making possible the giving of life to the world. The defeat of God's representative was the victory of God.

How did death bring life? How did defeat bring victory?

Here's where we have gotten confused and have tended to limit our message to issues of forgiveness of sins and life after death. We tell people that the cross means we are forgiven. Jesus has paid the penalty of our sins. And Jesus' resurrection means we will have life after death and be with God in heaven. That has been our message. But it has retained only two dimensions: we have neglected the good news about the kingdom in the here and now. The powerful experience and explanation of the inbreaking rule of God, in which people were being set free from sin, sickness and spiritual oppression and even the spirit of a nation was being changed, has been largely lost. We've replaced it with a much more individualistic message about freedom from guilt and fire insurance after we die.

This reduced message is neither biblical nor effectual. Christians have lost confidence in the gospel because we have lost crucial elements of the gospel. We have replaced the good news of the dynamic, transforming, inbreaking rule of God to set all things right with the somewhat static and stale message of the death and resurrection of Jesus to set a couple of things right for individuals who believe. In particular, the reduced good news is about dealing with guilt and securing our future destiny after we die, and receiving a domesticated Jesus who meets all our needs.

How do we recover a more full, dynamic and biblical understanding of the good news, so that it once again functions as good and as news, for believers and for seekers?

A NEW ANGLE OF VISION

Along with N. T. Wright and others, I suggest that the biggest missing piece in our understanding of the gospel has to do with our angle of vision. We have misunderstood the writings of the apostle Paul because we have not been able to see things from his angle of vision. And we have misunderstood the message of Jesus because we have not been able to see things from his angle of vision. The basic thread that holds Jesus and Paul together, and the angle of vision we most need to recover, is what biblical scholars call apocalyptic, or eschatological, vision.

When Jesus proclaimed the advent of God's rule to set things right, the people of his day understood him to mean that the final days of God's judgment and harvest had come. The nation of Israel, and then the nations of the world, would be judged, and the rule of God would be established. The world would now work as it had been meant to. The lion would lie down with the lamb, swords would be beaten into plowshares, and God's just peace would rest upon planet Earth and even upon the surrounding cosmos. You wonder why many Jewish people don't see Jesus as the Messiah? It is because Israel wasn't liberated, sin and evil weren't eradicated, and the nations did not immediately turn and worship God. Those events were all part of Jewish people's expectations for the coming of the Messiah and the advent of God's reign.

From the point of view both Jesus and Paul had, God chose a very surprising way to inaugurate and then expand his rule. But for both Jesus and Paul, the end times had now been seeded into history, and if you had eyes to see, transformation—individual, social and national—was all around you. The smallest of all seeds, the kingdom life, teachings and death of Jesus, was now planted and growing and would become the greatest of all bushes.

The core of the story is the death and resurrection of Jesus. But how do the death and resurrection of Jesus activate the dynamic rule of God to set all things right?

JUDGMENT AND HARVEST

The reporters of the news of Jesus' death interpreted what Jesus' death meant and accomplished in light of the climax of all of history. The end of time had entered into the middle of time. The judgment and harvest of the nations, and especially of the nation of Israel, which the prophets and seers had announced, was now happening before the eyes of all who saw Jesus go to the cross. Jesus wasn't guilty. But Israel was, and Jesus had identified with Israel in its sin. Already in his baptism he had identified with Israel, and then he fulfilled that identification in his death. And so God judged Israel, and the nations, at the cross. Whoever identifies with Jesus has already died with him (see Romans 6:1-14). Judgment has occurred. Sin has been dealt with. For one who is in Christ, now that the nails have been pounded in, and the cross has been raised, and the curse of hanging on a tree has fallen, there is no final judgment day left to face. Judgment has fallen, and the sentence has been served. We shall be judged for what we do with the good news we have been given, but we never have to face a final judgment for what we were without Christ.

Did you ever realize that you have already experienced the final judgment day? When people, even scholars, talk about the death of Jesus on the cross, most of us use the courtroom analogy merely as a metaphor. *It's more than a metaphor.* We who are in Christ have already stood before the judgment bar of God and been accepted, because in Christ we are on the other side of Judgment Day. And in Christ, the resurrection of our body and being has been sealed by the gift of the Spirit of God. The Holy Spirit is the down payment of full and complete restoration and resurrection. Transformation of individuals and societies and all creation has begun because the Holy Spirit of God has been given.

This end-times angle of vision is the key to understanding how Jesus' message of the kingdom of God and Paul's message about salvation are really one and the same. Paul understands that justification, or God's declaring us right and just, has happened: the final judgment day is in the past, having happened at the cross for all those in Christ. Yet salvation is not only in the past. It is an ongoing reality of transformation (sanctification) by the Spirit of God that will lead to fulfillment (glorification) in the resurrection of our bodies and beings and the renewal of all creation. Salvation is past, present and future. We have been justified; we are being sanctified; we shall be glorified. All these acts of God are dimensions of God's salvation. Salvation is the inbreaking and dynamic rule of God to set all things right.

SO WHAT'S THE STORY?

At the heart of this great news is a story that purports to be the main plotline of history. We need to recapture the story of God's great reclamation project to set all things right. Here's the big-picture view, starting with a big bang:

- God made the universe, and God loves what God has made. Whether God made it in a big bang at the beginning of time or in some other way, God made it all. Everything that is belongs to its Creator.

- God made human beings in God's image, with capacities to reason, love, relate and rule. Whether God made us through the process of evolution or in some other way, we are accountable to God for what we do with the capacities for good and evil, love and hate, that we have been given.

- Human beings lost their innocence, choosing to become independent from God and to set themselves up as their own god. Whether that happened in primeval times or happens now in individual lives, human beings chose and choose to use their freedom to serve themselves rather than serving God, others and all creation. The end result of this fall from innocence is the disintegration of all human societies, their tendency toward self-destruction, injustice and violence.

- God loves humanity passionately and has mounted several restoration projects. God first chose Israel to be God's people, the channel of God's love and justice for the world. When Israel proved to be like any other nation, going its own way and descending into idolatry and injustice, God sent God's Son.

- Jesus is God's Son, God "in the flesh," showing us the full capacity of God-filled humanity to love God, others and all creation.

- Jesus went to death, even a humiliating death on a cross, to take the just judgment on all human beings and on all nations for the sin and self-centeredness of humanity. God has judged all humanity at the cross. God's judgment, which we thought was reserved for the end of time, has happened in the middle of time!

- Jesus rose from the dead, paving the way into the final transformation of all humanity to be like Jesus. God will raise all humanity at the end of time. Those who are in Christ will receive the destiny of Christ, and those who have rejected Christ will have condemned themselves already. We have a picture in Christ of the final transformation and destiny of all things.

- God poured out God's Spirit on all followers of Jesus at Pentecost and ever since, inaugurating the union with Christ that will be fulfilled in all nations at the end of time. That union cuts across race, gender, class and culture and begins the uniting of all things in Christ in the here and now.

- We can personally enter God's rule to set all things right through turning from the self's way to God's way and placing our faith in Jesus. We trust Jesus for forgiveness through the cross, commit ourselves to Jesus' leadership for every part of life, are baptized as a sign of our union with Christ and our incorporation into the church, and receive the gift of the Holy Spirit. The Holy Spirit makes us one with God and inaugurates transformation in our individual, communal and national lives, as we cooperate. This transformation process, begun now, will be completed when we are raised from the dead and glorified to be like Jesus in his resurrected life. Then the systems and nations of this world will fully become the kingdom of our God.

Salvation is the restoration of God's gracious rule, in the past, present and future, for individuals, communities, nations and all creation.

Salvation is spiritual *and* physical. The gifts of the forgiveness of sins and union with God through the Holy Spirit affect our body and our being, our soul and spirit. No part of us is left unchanged when God comes to us, forgives us and fills us.

Salvation is individual *and* communal. The Spirit does not just re-create individuals. The Spirit fills the whole community, creating us as a body. We are mystically connected, united and changed. We cannot come to God and remain isolated individuals. It is not a matter merely of whether we join the church or not. With forgiveness of sins and union with Christ through the gift of the Spirit, we are already connected to the kingdom community.

Salvation is personal *and* social. The Holy Spirit is the leaven in the lump of human history that is transforming society. By the Spirit, we are connected to the poor, to people of other races and to Christ followers in every nation. The Spirit within us calls us to live out the unity that has already been established between us.

Salvation is human *and* cosmic. God's intention was that humanity would use its capacities to rule and steward creation. As we are forgiven and made one with Christ by being filled with the Spirit, that intention is renewed in our inner and corporate lives in ways that begin to influence even nature.

Salvation is for people *and* nations. When Jesus called his followers to go out and tell the world the great news about God's inbreaking rule to set all things right (Matthew 28:19-20), Jesus sent them not just to individuals but to nations. Jesus called them to disciple and teach nations. Even the life of nations would be changed by this news. And throughout history, nations have been changed as the good news has been proclaimed and embraced.

That's *good*. And that's *news*.

Stories shape our identity. And *the* Story, God's story, is the fundamental identity-shaping story for followers of Christ. So let's pursue knowing and telling the Story, first of all for ourselves as a way of deepening our own identity in Christ.

Can you tell this story? Where does this story touch known human history? Where does this story intersect with your story? Do you know who you are?

SHARING THE GOOD NEWS

In addition to knowing the Story, how can we share it with others? How did people in Scripture, like Paul, Peter and Jesus himself, share the good news of God's inbreaking rule to set all things right?

- The theme of the good news, the plotline that gives the story its meaning and importance, ought always to be the dynamic action of God to set all things right. The good news is not just about forgiveness or heaven or any other individual benefit, but about the transformation of individuals, communities and the whole cosmos into all that God originally intended.

- Evangelism is always about communicating God's rule to set all things right in the person of Jesus. Jesus, the events of Jesus' life and Jesus' presence here and now are always the *content* and the focus of the *experience* of the good news.

- Every gospel encounter is a power encounter or authority encounter. The crucial issue is always the authority of Jesus. Will we respond to Jesus on his terms or only on our own? In every age, people encounter the truth about Jesus and the reality of Jesus and must respond to his authority. His first hearers were amazed because he taught as one having authority and not as the teachers and the scribes.

- Jesus' authority addresses people at points of felt need, but it also addresses people at points of resistance, rebellion, self-centeredness and personal autonomy. The heart of the matter is always our response to the authority of Jesus.

At the end of the day, people who give their full allegiance to Jesus will be led by Jesus into all that he wants them to know, be and do. People need to hear of and experience the love and authority of Jesus for the world and for their life, and respond on Jesus' terms, not their own. I had to do that. You had to do that.

People helped me to do that by telling me about Jesus' love for and authority over me: his authority to forgive sins, lead people, free and heal people from addiction and sickness, and transform people and nations until everything has been set right.

We can help others by telling Jesus' story and letting them know of his love for them and his authority.

In order for people to hear and experience the message, we must start where they are. We can't just launch in and follow our script. We must start where people are and lead them through the story of Jesus' love and authority. Appendix one gives you a lot of help in learning how to engage others in conversation about God's story.

People know that life is not as it ought to be. The vision of life restored and renewed is a very compelling message today. It is truly good news!

8

INVITATION TO A WEDDING
Journey Versus Event

I met MaryKay when I began my new job in Madison, Wisconsin. She and I worked for the same organization for several years. We didn't get on very well. She thought I was uptight and judgmental. I could tell she didn't like me much, and so I returned the favor.

At one staff meeting, our mutual supervisor told us to both stand. We weren't sure why, and neither were the rest of the staff. Our mutual dislike was common knowledge, and so one of our colleagues quipped, "What? Are they getting married?" Everybody laughed, except for MaryKay and me. Our looks at our mischievous colleague could have carried daggers.

Our supervisor then announced it was our birthday. Thus MaryKay and I discovered that we had been born in the same year and on the same day! We traded driver's licenses because we couldn't believe it. When I looked at her license and saw the same birth date as mine, I thought it must be some kind of joke. But it wasn't. On October 24, all those years ago, she in Wisconsin and I in California had entered the world a mere eighteen hours apart (I was older, a fact that I have never let her forget!).

After this, we finally decided that we should do something to melt the ice between us. We worked for the same organization, we were both followers of Jesus, we shared a birth date—we ought to at least try to like each other a little. So we went disco dancing! We had a great time.

A couple of months later, after we'd taken a few more steps toward becoming friends, she called one night to ask if I wanted to meet her at the movies. I asked her what time. She told me to meet her in about an hour, if I was available. Now that was sad for me. It happened that I was hosting twelve students, with whom I was working at the University of Wisconsin, Madison; I had invited them over for a spaghetti dinner and an evening of conversation and relationship building. The noodles were simmering on the stove, and the students had gathered and were just warming up for the evening.

I looked at the phone with disappointment, then raised it to tell MaryKay the discouraging news. "Sure, that sounds great! See you in an hour," I heard myself say. Something was going on in my heart that I hadn't recognized. The friendship was starting to matter to me a little more than I had realized.

I fed those students spaghetti, packed them into a couple cars, drove them back to campus and arrived at the movie theater right on time. Of course, I didn't tell MaryKay what it had taken to pull it off. I was still trying to play it cool.

Three months later, MaryKay and I had the DTR talk. For those of you who have been out of the dating scene for a while, DTR stands for "define the relationship." The DTR talk started out poorly. MaryKay and I were leading a seminar together. At the lunch break, MaryKay apologized to me for speaking of me negatively to other people. I will never forget her words! "Rick," she started, "you may think I hate you." Now, I wasn't thinking she hated me. I thought we were doing pretty well. But if she thought I might think that she hated me, maybe she did.

So I asked her, "MaryKay, what are you so afraid of?"

She described later what happened to her at that moment. She looked up and, in her mind's eye, saw the clouds part, revealing the three words "I like you." What she said to me was, "I think I like you." And then she flushed in embarrassment, and even a little mortification. She was not expecting to ever like me in *that* way. She wasn't sure she wanted to. But there it was. Her heart had run in that direction, and she now was having to face it.

Now I was reeling. She had started the conversation by trying to assure me she didn't hate me, which hadn't even occurred to me until she brought it up. Now all of a sudden she was telling me she wanted to explore a romantic relationship.

It took me about a week to recover from the successive shocks, and then we began to date. Six months later, I popped the question out on the Arizona desert at sunset, when we were visiting my parents over Thanksgiving break. And six months after that we were married in Madison at our little Episcopal church. The rest, as they say, is history.

I wish I could say that after our rocky start it's all been smooth sailing since. But we are both strong personalities and have our opinions and needs. We are a lot like Aravis and Cor in C. S. Lewis's Narnia story *The Horse and His Boy.* Lewis says of them that they would fight and make up, and then fight and make up, until finally they got married so as to go on doing it more conveniently. And I wouldn't have it any other way. It's been great for me to be married to a partner and companion and equal like MaryKay.

Why do I share this story, and at some length? Did I just change the subject, jumping from the "religious" topic of conversion to the relational topic of marriage? Not at all. Rather, I want to suggest that we need to switch from an image of conversion as "doing something religious" to an image of conversion as doing something relational, like getting married.

The predominant and unifying image of salvation in Scripture is *union with Christ*. Conversion is union, a relational and spiritual marriage of our soul with God's Spirit. There are many parallels between this union with God and union in marriage with another person.

Marriage is the culmination of a process that includes friendship, courtship, meeting the family, engagement, a marriage ceremony and a honeymoon night (which too often these days happens well before the marriage ceremony!). In our sales and business model of conversion, what is crucial is making the sale and focusing on the bottom line. We even focus a lot on our "profit margin," the cost of our ministry relative to the number of conversions. In a relational model of conversion, what is important is not "sales figures" but growth into intimacy, commitment and union.

If one great image of us as witnesses is a travel guide, another great image is matchmakers! When we speak about Jesus, we are trying to introduce people to the Person who will become their one and only, the love of their life.

Marriage includes crucial crisis events. People have to decide to get to know one another and spend time. Someone has to initiate the DTR talk. Someone later has to "pop the question." People have to commit themselves to one another, first privately, but then publicly, before their community. The marriage has to be consummated, and then people have to begin to journey together and make a common life.

These contemporary American steps are not universal. In some cultures, marriages are arranged. But the principle—that there are key moments of decision and crisis in a larger process of relational commitment and growth—is universal.

Conversion is like marriage to a person in another important way. In marriage, we do not just join another person; we join their family too. So it is with conversion to God. We join and are joined to God's family. That's one reason baptism is so very important. Baptism marks publicly our union to Christ, but also our union with God's family. Conversion is not just a "me and God" thing. Conversion is a family affair.

So conversion, like marriage, is best seen as a larger relational process with milestone events along the way. There is the decision to become intentional in the spiritual search. There is a decision to get to know more about Jesus and to begin to try to relate to Jesus. Often someone has to "pop the question" of commitment. And then there is a crisis moment of decision to trust and commit oneself to Jesus as forgiver and leader. But the parallels don't end there. As in marriage, there is a public declaration of that mutual commitment before the community. In Scripture, this public event is always baptism. That leads to beginning to build the relationship and make a life together.

Many of our confusions about conversion could be dispelled if we realized that the best human analogy of conversion is marriage. Remember, the apostle Paul turns to the analogy of marriage when he talks about the relationship of Christ to the church (see Ephesians 5, for instance). The reason this analogy is so revealing is that salvation is best understood as union with God.

Conversion is also a change in allegiance from other things and people to Jesus. It is a response to the good news about Jesus and his kingdom. It is an authority encounter with Jesus in which we finally accept the authority of Jesus on his terms rather than ours.

Our personal experiences of conversion vary: we change our allegiance and experience that union through different steps taken in different sequence, depending on our background, life events and the unique way the Holy Spirit works in our life. So what is conversion exactly? When does it occur? How do we invite others into conversion?

WHAT DOES THE BIBLE
SHOW AND TELL US ABOUT CONVERSION?

The dimensions of conversion in Scripture are fairly clear. The best source is Acts, because this book shows many clear examples of people, Jewish and Gentile, men and women, young and old, individuals and whole households, Greek and Roman, all becoming followers of Jesus. The first recorded evangelistic sermon and response is a fairly typical illustration of the dimensions of conversion.

After his death and resurrection Jesus spent forty days with the apostles, showing them many proofs that he was really alive. Apparently they needed a lot of reassurance on this one! They wanted Jesus to tell them when Israel would be liberated and restored to supremacy. Jesus made it clear that the timeline and even the question were not what they needed to focus on. He had a job for them, a mission. They would now proclaim the good news about the in-breaking rule of God to set all things right, first in Jerusalem. Then they would fan out from there, ultimately going to all the nations. God's rule would advance heart by heart and nation by nation. And Jesus told them not to run out and get busy but to wait for power from the Holy Spirit. Right from the beginning, Jesus' way was the way of collaboration. So they waited.

After forty days Jesus stopped appearing. About ten days later, they were praying and waiting, and the Holy Spirit was poured out in dramatic and public fashion. People watching were amazed and confused. Were these disciples drunk, or was this event a miracle?

Peter begins to address the crowd, which is now intrigued and confused, some wondering and some ridiculing. He explains this outpouring of the Holy Spirit as the promised end-times act of God to save all people. In the last chapter, we considered how Jesus' death was God's act to judge all nations, not at the end of history but in the middle. Now the pouring out of the Spirit to create worship and unify people of different nations, genders, ages and cultures was another end-times event brought into the middle of history.

Then Peter speaks about Jesus. After briefly reviewing his miracles and death, Peter spends most of his time talking about God's vindication of Jesus by raising Jesus from the dead. "God has made this Jesus, whom you crucified, both Lord and Christ." He confronts the people with their terrible sin of crucifying Jesus and with the challenging authority and lordship of Jesus. They are "cut to the heart" and ask what they should do. Peter tells them: "Repent and be baptized, every one of you, in the name of Jesus Christ for the forgiveness of your sins. And you will receive the gift of the Holy Spirit" (see Acts 2:1-41).

Based on this passage, biblical conversion includes several dimensions:

- repentance
- faith in Jesus (notice the phrase "in the name of Jesus")
- baptism and incorporation into the community
- forgiveness of sins
- the gift of the Holy Spirit

If you explore scriptural passages about conversion, you will notice these dimensions again and again. The Gospel of John combines repentance and faith into "believing in Jesus." In the book of

Acts, every time conversion stories are told these dimensions are present, explicitly or implicitly.

Let's take note of some very important and often neglected biblical implications for conversion.

Conversion involves more than intellectual assent to some ideas. It involves a change of heart and mind from self-rule to God's rule.

Faith means much more than we have often understood. Today we tend to see faith as either intellectual assent or emotional optimism. But biblically, faith is a whole-person response to Jesus. It is incorporation into the name of Jesus, into his person, character and ways. So faith has intellectual, emotional, moral and volitional dimensions. We choose to *believe that* (intellectual aspect) Jesus was God in the flesh who has died for our sins and risen to be our Lord. We *trust* (emotional aspect) Jesus and put our whole weight on him for life. We *confess* (moral aspect) sin and self-centeredness and embrace Jesus' way of love and justice as our way. And we *choose* (volitional aspect) to follow Jesus in his way of life and his mission.

Further, notice that conversion is not just something individuals do. The church is part of genuine conversion. Conversion is not conversion unless there is a communal recognition of it through baptism and incorporation into the community.

Finally, conversion is the human side of initiation into God's rule to set all things right. But God is still the main actor in genuine conversion. God forgives sins because of what Jesus has done on the cross. And God gives the gift of the Holy Spirit, who makes us one with God. The Holy Spirit then empowers transformation and witness to the people and nations of the world.

Although for most people in the biblical accounts all these events happened in close proximity time wise, in our lives these different dimensions may happen at different points. Gordon Smith in his book *Beginning Well* helps us to affirm and embrace this diversity by clarifying conversion as follows: "Conversion is best thought of as a protracted experience that involves several distinct elements or events that each person will experience in a different way and in a different sequence, reflecting the unique manner in which the Holy Spirit of God is at work in his or her life."

To summarize, then:

Conversion is union with God and initiation into the rule of God, who is setting all things right.

Our part in conversion is repentance and faith. *Repentance*, not a commonly used word, means turning around and changing our mind. We turn from self to God and from self's way to God's way. You can look at faith in terms of its intellectual, affective, moral and volitional dimensions. What must we know, feel, confess and commit ourselves to?

The church's part in conversion is baptism and inclusion in God's family.

God's part in conversion is the forgiveness of sins and the gift of the Holy Spirit.

THE ANALOGY OF MARRIAGE: POPPING THE QUESTION

Marriage usually happens only after someone pops the question, "Will you marry me?" and the other person says, "Yes!" In some cultures, the question might be popped parent to parent. But someone still needs to do it.

Union with God most often has the same precursor—someone pops the question. "Do you want to follow Christ and commit your life to God?" What a joy to be part of the matchmaking and journey-guide process at this point of initiation! But many of us

never expect God to use us that way, never ask for that kind of opportunity and rarely notice it when the opportunity comes.

One close friend of mine attended my church for several
months, all the time wanting someone to explain how to come into
a relationship of commitment and closeness to God. She attended
services, tried out a small group, came to classes and seminars, all
the time wanting someone to invite her into relationship with God.
Finally, in exasperation, she cornered the pastor of the church and
asked straight out, "How do I become a Christian?" He was so
shocked and flustered that it took him a couple of days to get back
to her!

The first person who ever asked me how to become a Christian
got an even poorer response than that friend did from our pastor.
We were having a seekers small group, and at the first study my
friend Scott said, "OK, Rick. This is great, but how do I do it?"

"How do you do what?" I responded.

"How do I get God in my life?" Scott clarified.

After several attempts that failed miserably, I handed him a
booklet that hopefully would explain it better than I was ready to.

Scott called me the next day, "Rick, I did it!" he exclaimed, a
note of joy and excitement in his voice.

"That's fantastic, Scott," I shot back. "So what exactly did you
do?" Scott went on to explain to me how one becomes a follower
of Jesus!

Later in my journey with Jesus, I was leading another seeker
small group. One of the two members seemed to me to be far
from ready to respond to Jesus. The other one was already a follower of Jesus, as far as I could tell. My pastor challenged me to
pop the question. I didn't want to, because I didn't think it fit their
location on the journey. One guy might be insulted because he al-

ready was committed to Jesus; the other guy might be pushed further away. But sensing the nudge of the Spirit in the challenge of my pastor—and if I'm honest, also wanting to prove my pastor was missing the mark—I summarized the gospel story and asked where they saw themselves in the process of trusting Christ. To my shock, chagrin and happiness, all at the same time, both responded that they hadn't ever really responded to the authority of Jesus, but wanted to. I proceeded to prompt them into a commitment to union with Christ!

Have you ever popped the question? Do you want to? Or do you want to be like I was for a long time, mentoring people up to the point of commitment and then waiting around until somebody else got the enjoyment of popping the question and seeing people respond?

BOUNDED SET VERSUS CENTERED SET, JOURNEY VERSUS EVENT

There are many ways in which conversion is like marriage to another person. But there is a crucial way in which conversion is very different. In conversion, we become one with a Person who is invisible! There is always a moment of union, when God by God's Holy Spirit becomes one with a human person, but there is no way for those of us who watch to know when that actually happens. Yet we spend so much time trying to figure out who is "saved" and who is not, who is "in" and who is "out," and whom we can count. A couple of other ways to look at conversion can help you (1) know how you can be helpful to others and (2) stop asking that question of who is in and who is out, and leave it to God.

If conversion is a process that involves time and multiple dimensions of our selves, and happens in people in different ways given their background, experience and the unique work of the Holy Spirit in their life, then deciding who is a Christian and who is not becomes not only difficult but impossible. If lots of people are "on the way," then the crucial question is not "Are you in or are you out?" but rather, "What direction are you going?" That's a question you and I can ask as good matchmakers and travel guides.

Paul Hiebert, an anthropologist, has put words to what many of us have felt. He points out that we tend to think in terms of *bounded sets*. Where is the boundary, and what side of the boundary are you on? Hiebert encourages us to think of *centered sets*. In this case the crucial question changes: What direction are you moving, and what is your relationship with the center of the set?

Not only does centered-set thinking help us, but so does the image of journey. For followers of Jesus, the center is not static. Jesus is moving, and the crucial question is "Are you following?"

These are questions we can ask, and people can often respond to them meaningfully. Appendix two pictures these various models of conversion.

Post-Christian people don't want to hear the question popped in cliché ways and with a one-size-fits-all approach. And they will be offended if it seems as if you need them to respond more than they want to respond. Evangelism is not about sales but about spiritual guidance. It's not about getting "in" instead of being "out." It's similar to getting married, becoming one with the God who loves us and will transform us. So let's not ask post-Christian people to mark their choice with trite responses. Prompt them to use their own words and to mark their initiation in a significant and meaningful way. The biblical pattern is to be baptized in a very public ceremony.

Your main Christian leadership may be in a parachurch group that doesn't baptize. In that case, celebrate commitments in public ways, and then encourage new initiates to be baptized in the church community of their choice.

PROMPTING A COMMITMENT

How do we help people into initiation into God's rule and into union with Christ?

We learn to tell the gospel story and ask good questions, as explored in previous chapters (also see appendix one). And then we invite people to respond when they are ready, helping them find the time, the place and the words that will express their heart and respond to what the Holy Spirit is doing in their life.

Here are questions we can ask:

- Where are you in the process of trusting Christ? Is there any reason you couldn't ask for his forgiveness and leadership right now?

- Are you open to joining Jesus' community and Jesus' cause to transform you and your world? Is there anything holding you back?

- Are you interested in asking God to fill you with God's presence to change you and give you strength to follow Jesus?

- Would you want to pray with me now, or talk to God on your own later?

Then, if they are ready and want to respond with us, we can prompt them in finding their own words.

Here's how Sharon—a shy and introverted woman, not very good at sales, but a wonderful travel guide—led Alicia recently through a conversational response to God.

Sharon prayed, "Thank you, God, for working in Alicia's heart. Thank you that she wants to follow you, Jesus. Help her now to have words to share her heart with you, God." Then Sharon said to Alicia, "Why don't you just ask God in your own words to forgive you and help you turn away from living for yourself and help you to live for God?"

Alicia prayed, "God, I just want to know you. Please forgive me for the ways I've ignored you and hurt others. Especially help me with my relationship with Rob."

Sharon then encouraged her: "Now just let Jesus know you want him to be your leader and to come into your life and take the driver's seat." They had talked about that image of asking Jesus to be in the driver's seat earlier.

Alicia prayed, "Jesus, I want you to take charge of my life. I want to know you and learn what you want me to do. Help me, God."

Sharon prayed, "God, thank you so much for giving Alicia the desire to follow you. Now God, I ask for you to forgive her completely and fill her with your presence." Then Sharon prompted her, "Alicia, why don't you in your own words ask to be filled with God's presence, with God's Holy Spirit?"

"Yes, God, fill me with your Spirit. I need you so much. I commit myself to you."

Sharon closed their prayer time by praying, "Thank you, God, for Alicia's commitment to you. Thank you that you promise to forgive us, lead us and fill us when we ask. Alicia has asked. Thank you for Alicia. I like her so much, and I know you love her to pieces. Now strengthen her to follow you and join you in serving others. Amen."

Sharon gave Alicia a big hug. And she encouraged her to consider telling her small group what had happened. A few months later, she was baptized before the whole church. Alicia beamed with joy that day. And so did Sharon!

Don't you want to be part of popping the question and inviting people into the kingdom? Have you had that experience?

"You do not have because you do not ask" (James 4:2).

CONCLUSION

I end this chapter on conversion as marriage and us as matchmakers by popping some questions to you.

Will you commit yourself to becoming a more vibrant witness in the days to come?

Can you see yourself as a travel guide instead of a traveling salesperson? Can you pursue spiritual conversations with friends on the journey?

Will you become a better detective, looking for clues of God's Spirit at work in the lives of others? Can you become a better collaborator and partner with God in witness?

Could you give up a cookie-cutter approach to what a witness looks like, and instead contribute your particular gifts to the witness of the whole community?

Could you do what you love with people who don't know Jesus yet? Could you share with them your struggles and doubts and spiritual failures? Will you learn to minister to wounded hearts?

Can you learn to tell good transformation stories for each stage of your life? Can you talk about the real experiences and encounters you've had with the presence and authority of God?

Can you begin to talk about Jesus in some surprising and "rock my world" ways? Would you be willing to challenge the spiritual consumerism that is rampant in our culture, and often in our own hearts?

Do you know the Big Story? Can you tell the story of God's love affair with humanity and God's reclamation project to transform the whole world? Do you know where you fit into God's story? Do you know who you are?

Will you grow in the art of spiritual matchmaking and begin to ask God for opportunities to pop the question?

As we together begin to embrace these new images of evangelism and live into these questions, I believe God could pour out the Spirit and bring great renewal to the church and to the world.

Will you join me on this journey? Far more to the point, will you join Jesus? I still hear him say: "As the Father sent me, so I send you."

APPENDIX 1

Building Trust in a Multiethnic World

Many people are looking for help with witness, not just in the dominant post-Christian Western culture but within other specific ethnic and cultural groupings. So I want to offer some reflections and stories that will help you begin to adapt this book to whatever cultural group you may be trying to reach. And I want to start by summarizing the theme and thrust of this book.

But before I get to that, let me note that the theme of this book has been building trust in a post-Christian society. Though I did not explicitly articulate that theme, it has informed all that I have written. I have challenged you, the reader, to see broken trust as an opportunity instead of a problem, a bridge instead of a barrier in your conversations and relationships with seekers and skeptics.

Why do we face such serious trust issues when we try to share our faith with those around us? Many of us live in a post-Christian society where there has been a breach of trust toward spiritual leaders and religious institutions. The Christian church has had immense influence and power in many cultures, and especially in the West. Wherever the church has had power and misused it, trust problems abound. In the distant past, for instance in the Crusades and the Inquisition, when the cross and the sword were united, violence toward the outsider and "the infidel" set in motion consequences that extend to the present day. In addition, when the church has had power and been silent in the face of injustice, as with the Holocaust, affected groups, like the Jewish people, have come to associate the cross with hatred and fear.

In contemporary postmodern Western culture, where the church has also had great influence and power, trust problems may be less obvious but often are still quite serious. I have sought in this book to help us learn to identify with broken trust by admitting that we experience it ourselves and by expressing our struggles to others authentically. Only then can we begin to minister to wounded hearts.

Beyond taking these direct steps to rebuild trust, we can let go of agendas and scripts, learn to collaborate with the Holy Spirit, practice spiritual hospitality, recount authentic stories of God's reality, tell the great news of God's transforming power in the here and now and forever, and be matchmakers in the dating-and-marriage dance between people and the God who loves them. All of these pursuits and images aim to rebuild bridges of trust that can carry the weight and freight of Christian truth.

The question that must propel us is, how can trust and truth walk hand in hand in our witness in a post-Christian world? We need to answer this question regardless of what culture or ethnic group we are in.

Similarly we must ask, what are people's trust issues regarding Christians, the church and God? Can I identify with those trust issues? Can I minister to wounded people? What are the boxes around Jesus and faith that need to be challenged and broken? How can I speak about Jesus in fresh, authentic and unexpected ways?

Whatever the cultural background, a person's trust issues often revolve around the way churches and leaders have used their power and authority. Trust can be broken by a misuse of power or by silence and passivity in the face of social evil. People can have broken trust toward pastors, churches, Christians and God. People often express broken trust toward God with the question "Where was God when . . . ?" Whenever we talk with people from a culture in which the church has had power, we will need to be attentive to issues of broken trust. Especially in post-Christian societies, where the church was once dominant but now is increasingly marginalized, we will need to become wise trust-builders if we want to be effective truth-tellers.

I begin with African American culture, because outside white culture, that is the culture with which I have most often engaged.

The black church has had immense power in African American culture. For many years it was the only "black-run and black-owned" institution in the community. Thus the black church has served as a social, political, spiritual and economic center for many black communities, especially in the past but still today as well. The black church met important needs. For instance, many people were affirmed and had a status that they didn't experience in the larger society. Further, many black churches still reflect dimensions of African faith expression in their styles of preaching, worship and hierarchy. A good example of the African influence on the black church can be found in Pentecostalism. Pentecostalism, the fastest-growing Protestant expression of Christian faith globally, has roots in the black church experience, for it emerged publicly first in the Azusa Street Revival in Los Angeles in 1904 under the leadership of African American William Seymour. Pentecostal practices of ecstatic worship, speaking in tongues, healing and deliverance probably have their roots in the black churches during slavery; they represent a combination of an African spiritual worldview, an experience of suffering and oppression, and a genuine conversion to biblical faith. The long history and influence of the black church are to be celebrated. But the immense power and influence of the black church in the black community has also produced broken trust, probably especially among younger black men.

Fred, a young African American man, explored some of his trust issues with me recently. Having grown up in the church, he has questions about the emotionalism of the church in which he grew up. His perception is that some women of the church express their spiritual ecstasy during the service in ways that draw attention to themselves and with an almost predictable timing. He also has questions about the pastor's use of authority and his relationships with some women in the church. Further, he said, the messages from the pulpit focus on survival, suffering and emotional catharsis but don't seem to help people change, move forward or look ahead. Finally, dynamics of envy and jealousy within the church have affected him and his family in very negative ways.

Fred also expressed some of his trust issues with more traditional mainline black denominations, like the National Baptists and the African Methodist Episcopal denomination. Although these groups have often been at the forefront of political activism, Fred thinks they seem stuck in an older model that is not very relevant to economic, cultural and global realities today. They also seem less spiritually vibrant and are often not very affirming toward the leadership roles of women.

Fred knows enough history to understand the rationale for many of these practices and patterns, but the church has lost his trust. Yet he remains interested in spiritual questions.

Fred has also read some of the writings of black Muslims, like Malcolm X, who called Christianity the white man's religion. He notes that the white church justified slavery and segregation and preached a gospel of individual salvation that seemed to leave whites with their social sins unrecognized and unconfessed, to the detriment of African Americans.

So Fred has trust issues with both his own black church traditions and the church traditions of whites. As a white ethnic person, I was especially able to address the second set of trust issues. I told Fred about my relationship with Ronald V. Myers Sr., an African American who in the early 1980s was a medical student at the University of Wisconsin. Ron's first prayer for me was "Lord, I pray for my brother. He wants to help. He has a good heart. But he doesn't understand me, my people or our history. Lord, not only does he not understand, but he doesn't even understand that he doesn't understand. Lord, forgive him and help him." At first I was hurt. Then I realized Ron was right! That prayer launched a twenty-five-year friendship and partnership in ministry.

When I recounted that experience to Fred, his heart melted. Though he had huge trust issues with whites, my story of being an ignorant white brother but wanting to do something about it opened up my vulnerability and helped him engage with me at a new level. When I later shared with Fred the good news of God's salvation for individuals and societies, he was very interested to hear about this good news that speaks not only to individual transformation but also to social transformation and justice.

These sorts of trust issues are relevant in witness not only to African Americans but also to many other ethnic and cultural groups. When I have talked with Native Americans or First Nations people, I have found severe trust issues toward white churches and assimilationist Native American churches because of the U.S. history of first annihilating Native Americans and then radically rejecting the Native American culture and its more spiritual worldview.

When I have engaged with Latino Americans, I have often encountered trust issues toward white churches for their complete lack of awareness regarding Latino issues. In addition, many Latinos in the United States and overseas have trust issues with non-Catholics. Catholic-background Latinos are afraid that evangelicals are trying to convert them to Protestantism and take them away from their religious and cultural identities. These trust issues are rooted in the historical animosity between Catholics and Protestants in Latin America. So anti-Catholic approaches will reinforce and deepen broken trust.

With people with Asian ethnic roots, I have encountered mixed responses depending on how much power the church has had in any particular culture. For instance, when I have talked with Asian Americans with Korean ethnic roots, where the church has had a lot of power, I have encountered trust issues toward pastors and other leaders with Christian authority. Especially if a Korean American is second generation or later and has become bicultural or Americanized, he or she may have trust issues toward the style of exercising authority that many first-generation Koreans value.

Whenever we want to build bridges with people from different ethnic backgrounds, we need to be sensitive to trust issues they might have toward their own ethnic church tradition *and* trust issues they might have toward the dominant-culture church traditions. In a brief appendix I could never identify all the trust issues you might run into. But I can suggest a strategy of approach and a pattern of response:

- Keep your antennas up for prior questions of trust.
- Learn about and take responsibility for the ways people with

your own ethnic background may have hurt people from other ethnic backgrounds.

- Ask questions to explore how people may have trust issues with their own ethnic background church tradition.
- Identify with people where they've been hurt.
- Minister to their wounded hearts.
- Begin to speak truth and talk about Jesus in ways that break their stereotypes and rock their world.

You may not know the trust issues of the person you are talking to. But as you ask honest questions and listen as a learner, God can use you. Then you can better share Christ, and *you* may even write the next book to help us all! As you pursue this journey of rebuilding trust and speaking truth, I would love to hear about the trust issues you identify for the groups you are trying to reach. Building trust across racial and ethnic boundaries for the sake of the gospel is a lifelong commitment and passion for me, and I look forward to carrying on the conversation with you and many others in the days to come. You can let me know what you're learning at Rick.C.Richardson@wheaton.edu.

The Great News: The "What's at the Center?" Gospel Illustration

Here is an example of how you could share the Big Story of God's plan to reclaim and transform the world. I shared this illustration recently with a young woman with whom I had had several spiritual conversations. At an appropriate point in the relationship, I asked her: "You know, you and I have talked a lot about spiritual issues. I wonder if I could sort of summarize where I'm coming from and tell you the story of God's plan to heal the world."

I used an approach we are developing called the "What's at the Center?" Gospel Illustration. In the following diagrams, the inner circle represents individuals, the second circle represents relationships, and the outer circle represents systems, including institutions, ethnic groups, nations and even the whole natural world.

- You and I were made for good, as was everything that God created. It was all designed to have God at the center.

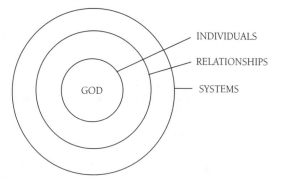

Figure 1. God at the center

This harmony with God at the center was meant not only for us as individuals but also for our relationships and even our structures of human and created existence. Things like racism and the gender wars and the greenhouse effect are not the way things are meant to be. So what went wrong?

- You and I have replaced God at the center with other things at the center, whether a relationship or a thing, like money or achievement or experiences. Ultimately we have put ourselves at the center. And not just you and I, but groups and cultures and nations have done that as well. We have been hurt by the resulting evil, and life is not as it should be, as we feel it could be.

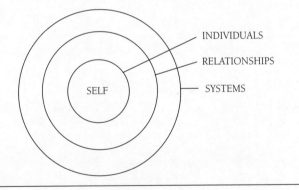

Figure 2. Self at center

We put ourselves at the center when we seek to run our own lives and look out for number one. Nations do that by seeking their own security and protection to the detriment of other nations. Races do that by putting themselves at the center and considering other races inferior. The end result of putting ourselves at the center is war. We all compete. We don't trust. We pull apart when we are hurt and wall ourselves off from others. We become lonely and are alienated from nature, others, God and even ourselves. At the core of who we are, we become spiritually dead, and our world becomes fragmented and embattled. God made us for good, and we owe God everything. We have chosen our own way instead of God's way and have reaped the painful consequences. Though God loves us, we have hurt and offended him because of how we have treated him. We deserve to be held accountable by God and to receive justice. We deserve to be alone and without God, spiritually dead, not only in this life but also in the next, because that's what we've chosen.

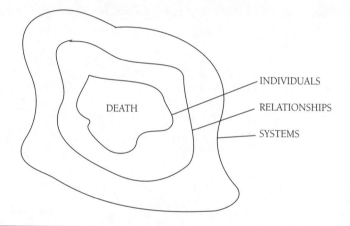

Figure 3. Spiritual death and a disinegrating world

I know that sounds kind of harsh. But there's also some really good news. God loved us, and the world, too much to leave us in this fix. He came to us as Jesus and showed us what a truly human and loving life looks like. He showed us what it would look like if all people were loved, if God's healing could come to all people, if harmony could be restored between men and women, between different races and nations, between humans and nature, and between us and God. And then Jesus died for us. He took our self-centeredness and its consequence, spiritual death, on himself at the cross. He paid the price of our self-centeredness so we don't have to. Jesus took on himself the judgment we deserve. His death for us is also a death for the self-centeredness of the whole world.

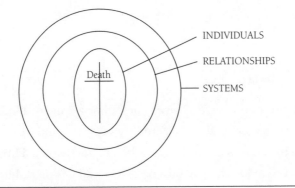

Figure 4. The cross at the center

Jesus by his death heals our relationship with God, but also begins the healing of our relationships with others and with the whole of creation. His death overcame our inner alienation from God. His death also begins the process of overcoming the alienation between races and classes and genders. God has begun healing the whole world.

- And Jesus not only died for us, but he also came back from the dead and is alive to give us life.

  His life makes us come alive, brings healing to our relationships and sets us free to join Jesus in his mission to heal the world.

- We need only respond. We *admit* our false centers and our self-centeredness and turn from them toward God. We *accept* Jesus' death for the death we deserve, for the hurt we have

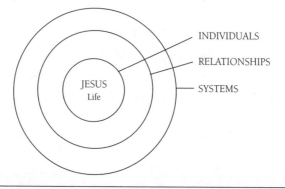

INDIVIDUALS

RELATIONSHIPS

SYSTEMS

JESUS
Life

Figure 5. Jesus at the center

caused and for the forgiveness that we need. Finally, we *ask*
Jesus to come into the center of our lives, and we commit ourselves to him as our forgiver, healer and leader. Through Jesus
our real identity—God's beloved child—is reestablished in relationship with God. And then we join Jesus in his mission to
heal the world and to invite individuals and groups to ask
Jesus to be in the center.

- Is God at the center of your life? Or is God somewhere else in
  your life, or even completely outside the circle of your life? Asking Jesus into the center of your life is like a marriage commitment, like adoption into a new family. You don't understand all
  that you are committing yourself to when you start, but you
  know it will affect everything else in your life for the rest of your
  life! Do you want God to be at the center of your life? Do you
  want to join Jesus in his mission to heal the world? Are you
  ready to take that step, or are you somewhere along the way?

If you are ready, you can have a simple conversation with
God to start that relationship. You too can respond and have
God as your center, your healer and forgiver and leader.

Here's how I led someone in that conversation recently. As I mentioned at the beginning, I was talking with a young woman recently. Her name was Leah. I began by praying, "Thank you, God, for working in Leah's heart. Thank you that she wants to follow you, Jesus. Help her now to have words to share her heart with you, God."

Then I said to Leah, "Why don't you just ask God in your own words to forgive you and help you turn away from living for yourself and help you to live for God?"

Leah prayed, "God, I just want to know you. Please forgive me for the ways I've ignored you and hurt others. Especially forgive me in my relationship with Rob."

I then encouraged her: "Now just let Jesus know you want him to be your leader and to come into your life and be at the center."

Leah prayed, "Jesus, I want you to come into my life, to be at the center. Help me, God."

I then prayed, "God, thank you so much for giving Leah the desire to follow you. Now God, I ask for you to forgive her completely and fill her with your presence." Then I prompted her, "Leah, why don't you in your own words ask to be filled with God's presence, and to join Jesus in his mission to heal others and the world?"

"Yes, God, fill me with your presence. I need you so much. I commit myself to you and to doing what I can to help in healing others."

I closed the prayer time by praying, "Thank you, God, for Leah's commitment to you. Thank you that you promise to forgive us, lead us and fill us when we ask. Leah has asked. Thank you for Leah. I like her so much, and I know you love her to pieces. Now strengthen her to follow you and join you in healing others. Amen."

Leah next told her small group she had invited God to be at the center of her life. A few months later, she was baptized before her church. Leah beamed with joy that day. And so did I!

APPENDIX 3

Models of Conversion

The following diagrams picture the bounded-set, centered-set and journey models of conversion. Many thanks to Brian McLaren in his book *More Ready Than You Realize* for these ideas.

First, here is a bounded-set picture of conversion, in which the key question is "Are you in or are you out?"

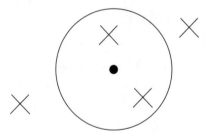

Next is a centered-set picture of conversion, where the key question becomes "Are you moving toward the center or away from it?"

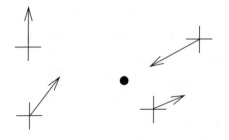

Finally, here is a journey model of conversion, where the key question is "Are you following in the footsteps of the leader or not?"

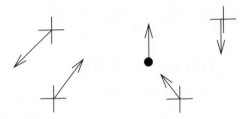

All three models together are better than any one alone, since "conversion is best thought of as a protracted experience that involves several distinct elements or events that each person will experience in a different way and in a different sequence, reflecting the unique manner in which the Holy Spirit of God is at work in his or her life."

Further, none of the models is an adequate basis for judging who is converted and who is not. Rather, these models give us questions we can ask people that can help them come to terms with their own relationship with God.

APPENDIX 4

Spiritual Gifts and Witness

PERSONAL REFLECTION

1. What do you think your spiritual gift (or gifts) might be? You can refer to the descriptions at the end of this appendix.

   - Organizing and leading
   - Evangelism and equipping
   - Hospitality and encouragement
   - Pasturing and teaching
   - Prayer, words and works from the Holy Spirit
   - Service and mercy
   - Giving

2. Where have you seen possible evidence for that gift in your life?

3. How could your gifts best contribute to the witness of the community?

4. Reflect on what your church would need to do to help you contribute. Do you need training? Do you need clarification of the corporate vision? Do you need a practical way to plug in? Reflect on what you most need, and what it would take for your church or community to provide it.

5. Have you ever asked to be filled with the Holy Spirit? Who do you respect that you could ask to lay hands on you and pray for you to be filled with the Holy Spirit?

GROUP DISCUSSION

Get into groups. Spend some time brainstorming about how you might use your gifts in your community for witness. Generate some ideas, and also talk about some of the barriers to fulfilling those ideas. What would it take for your church to effectively use you and your gifts in witness? What do you need in order to know how your gifts fit into the witness of your community? Choose a spokesperson to share what you generated with the whole group.

GIFT INVENTORY

- Organizing and leading
  1. When a job needs to get done, people often turn to me to lead and organize it.
  2. I like involving other people in tasks and projects.
  3. I believe that if the detailed preparations of an event don't get done, the event may fail.
  4. When I lead an event it often seems to go well.
  5. Whenever I attend an event I find myself evaluating how well it is going and how it could have been done better.
- Evangelism and equipping
  1. I enjoy being with people who don't follow Jesus yet.
  2. I have a lot of confidence in the power of the gospel.
  3. I have led at least one other person to Christ.
  4. I enjoy teaching and motivating other people to reach out.
  5. When we are planning an outreach event, other people turn to me for ideas about how to help people commit to Jesus.

- Hospitality and encouragement

    1. I enjoy having people in my home (or dorm room) for conversation and food.

    2. I enjoy creating spaces that are attractive and that help people feel comfortable.

    3. When a group I am involved with is planning an event, people turn to me for ideas to help others feel welcome and wanted.

    4. In group gatherings I notice the people who seem isolated or uncomfortable.

    5. When others at a group gathering are having a good time, I am happy.

- Pastoring and teaching

    1. I have led small groups before, and they have gone well.

    2. I enjoy asking people questions and finding out what they think.

    3. When people are in need I like to involve others in my community in meeting the need.

    4. I enjoy studying the Scriptures, and often see things that challenge and motivate me.

    5. I enjoy mentoring others.

- Prayer, words and works from the Holy Spirit

    1. When I see someone in need my first response is to tell them I will pray for them, and then to do it.

    2. When I pray for people I often feel like I connect with God and with them.

    3. I have had experiences of sensing from God what to pray for, and had people respond well.

4. I believe God heals people, and I pray for hurting people with the expectation that God will work.

5. I have prayed for people who don't yet follow Jesus.

- Service and mercy

  1. When I see someone in need my first urge is to do something practical to help them.

  2. I have been part of our church's efforts to serve the poor.

  3. I am upset when the church doesn't seem to care about people in need.

  4. I believe the best form of evangelism is to care about people in practical ways and let my actions do the talking.

  5. I have helped the church organize efforts to serve the poor here in the States or through an overseas mission trip.

- Giving

  1. I have some ability to make money.

  2. I enjoy giving to causes and efforts I believe in.

  3. When I see someone in need I want to help financially.

  4. I don't need to get the credit but only want to see the job get done.

  5. I want to invest in projects and people that really make an impact.

NOTES

Chapter 1: Reimagining Evangelism

p. 20   "In a short and simple conversation, Gandalf shows us the art": This conversation is taken from the movie *The Lord of the Rings: The Fellowship of the Ring*, scene 28, at 1:49:20-1:51:30 on the DVD. A similar conversation is found in the book by J. R. R. Tolkien, *The Fellowship of the Ring* (1965; reprint, New York: Ballantine, 1982), pp. 84-88.

p. 22   "Then they have a 'spiritual guidance' conversation": The dialogue is from the movie *The Lord of the Rings: The Fellowship of the Ring*, scene 32, at 2:20:35—2:23:10 on the DVD. The description is from Tolkien's *Fellowship of the Ring*, pp. 429-32.

p. 24   "Sam, this little hobbit, very simple and down to earth": This scene is from the movie *The Lord of the Rings: The Two Towers*, scene 50, at 2:43:45-2:46:40 on the DVD. A similar conversation takes place between Sam and Frodo in J. R. R. Tolkien's *The Two Towers* (1965; reprint, New York: Ballantine, 1982), pp. 406-9.

Chapter 2: Rediscovering the Holy Spirit

p. 36   "We should stop praying, 'Lord, bless what I'm doing' ": Rick Warren, *The Purpose Driven Church* (Grand Rapids: Zondervan, 1995), p. 15.

p. 38   "Evangelism as listening and partnering with the Holy Spirit": He tells an especially moving story of a Muslim's conversion through a dream while the Muslim was sleeping through York's sermon: R. York Moore. *Growing Your Faith by Giving It Away* (Downers Grove, Ill.: InterVarsity Press, 2005), pp. 30-40.

Chapter 3: The Witness of the Community

pp. 51-52   "Whenever people embrace a new identity": Brad Kallenberg draws especially on Ludwig Wittgenstein's insights into language to explore the function of community in conversion: Brad Kallenberg, *Live to Tell: Evangelism for a Postmodern Age* (Grand Rapids: Brazos, 2002), pp. 31-46.

p. 53   "Church has needed to reach pagan or non-Christian cultures": See George Hunter's *The Celtic Way of Evangelism: How Christianity Can Reach the West—Again* (Nashville: Abingdon, 2000), and my *Evangelism Outside the Box* (Downers Grove, Ill.: InterVarsity Press, 2000) for discussions of the place of community in the strategy of reaching pagan peoples.

p. 58   "I have identified six key gift areas": I am indebted to Mark Mittelberg and Bill Hybels for the idea that each of us has our own style of evangelism based on temperament, personality and gifting. Their focus was more individual; Hybels pointed out individuals using different styles of communication in different evangelistic encounters in the Scriptures. My starting point is the biblical material on spiritual gifts found in Romans 12, 1 Corinthians 12 and Ephesians 4, and my focus is to help people form *teams* and not just understand their individual style.

p. 62   "He later wrote, 'Ah, what a day!' ": Dwight L. Moody, quoted in Lyle W. Dorsett, *A Passion for Souls: The Life of D. L. Moody* (Chicago: Moody Press, 1997), p. 156.

p. 62   "God blessed him": Ibid.

p. 62   "Standing on the spectacular cliffs of St. Vincent": Pete Greig and Dave Roberts, *Red Moon Rising: How 24/7 Prayer Is Awakening a Generation* (Lake May, Fla.: Relevant Books, 2003), p. 1.

Chapter 4: The Art of Spiritual Friendship

p. 75   "She was coming to the well alone at noon": For a fascinating comparison, look at Genesis 24, which is the story of another woman at a well. Probably John has this story in mind as he writes about Jesus' encounter with the Samaritan woman at a well. Notice how Rebekah comes to the well at evening time in the company of many, is asked for water and gives it. She then waters all the camels, which would have taken immense time and immense amounts of water. The echoes in John 4 are strong, but even stronger are the contrasts. Both women are chosen, one because she is worthy, the other because of the new day Jesus has brought.

Chapter 5: The Power of Story

p. 84   "My friend Lon Allison": Lon Allison and Mark Anderson, *Going Public with the Gospel* (Downers Grove, Ill.: InterVarsity Press, 2003), p. 114.

pp. 84-85   "The reason that story is so basic": Eugene Peterson, *Leap over a Wall: Early Spirituality for Everyday Christians* (New York: Harper-Collins, 1997), pp. 3-4.

p. 86   "We have every little inconsequential thing": Sarah Hinckley, "Talking to Generation X," *First Things* 90 (February 1999): 11.

pp. 86-87   "Worldviews can be understood best": N. T. Wright, *The New Testament and the People of God* (Minneapolis: Fortress, 1992), pp. 132-33.

Chapter 6: Jesus Outside the Box

p. 101   "Jesus is more like Warhead candy": This analogy comes from Don Everts, author of the book *Jesus with Dirty Feet* (Downers Grove, Ill.: InterVarsity Press, 1999).

p. 105   *"Questions of community":* Rick Richardson, *Evangelism Outside the Box* (Downers Grove, Ill.: InterVarsity Press, 2000), pp. 38-40.

Chapter 7: Great News!

p. 122   "In his baptism he had identified with Israel": In Mark 1:9-12, Matthew 3:13-17 and Luke 3:21-22, Jesus seeks baptism. John objects, saying he is not worthy to baptize Jesus. From the context, it is clear Jesus doesn't personally need to be baptized for repentance and cleansing. So why is he baptized? Probably the key to understanding Jesus' baptism is in the moment when the Spirit descends on him and God says, "This is my beloved Son, in whom I am well pleased." In the Old Testament, God's beloved son was Israel, or the king who represented Israel. So here Jesus is the king who represents Israel. He is being baptized as a part of his identification with Israel and his representative kingship. Jesus is recapitulating the history of Israel, and this time it is done right.

Chapter 8: Invitation to a Wedding

p. 134   "The best source is Acts": For a similar perspective on conversion taken from the Gospel accounts, see Richard V. Peace, *Conversion in the New Testament* (Grand Rapids: Eerdmans, 1999).

p. 137   "Conversion is best thought of as a protracted": Gordon T. Smith, *Beginning Well: Christian Conversion and Authentic Transformation*

(Downers Grove, Ill.: InterVarsity Press, 2001), p. 138.

p. 140   "Paul Hiebert, an anthropologist": Paul G. Hiebert, "The Category of 'Christian' in the Mission Task," *International Review of Mission* 72 (July 1983): 421-27.

Appendix 2

p. 152   "Here is an example": Thanks to James Cheung for his outstanding work in developing a gospel illustration that takes seriously God's plan to reclaim the world. He has developed a narrative approach to sharing God's mission to heal the world and to inviting people to join him in that mission. James built on the "good news of the kingdom of God" approach advocated by Allen Wakabayashi in his book *Kingdom Come.* Thanks also to Andy Bilhorn for his suggestion of the three levels—personal, relational and systemic—for understanding the different dimensions of the impact of the gospel. The basic illustration of asking God to be at the center is taken from the "Circles of Belonging" gospel illustration in the booklet I authored by that name and also in my book *Evangelism Outside the Box,* both published by InterVarsity Press.

Appendix 3

p. 158   "Many thanks to Brian McLaren": Brian D. McLaren, *More Ready Than You Realize: Evangelism as Dance in the Postmodern Matrix* (Grand Rapids: Zondervan, 2002), pp. 137-40.

p. 159   "All three models together are better": Gordon T. Smith, *Beginning Well: Christian Conversion and Authentic Transformation* (Downers Grove, Ill.: InterVarsity Press, 2001), p. 138.

ABOUT THE AUTHOR

Rick Richardson is associate professor and director of the Masters in Evangelism program at Wheaton College. He is also associate national director for evangelism with InterVarsity Christian Fellowship. Formerly, he was pastor of evangelism and small groups at Church of the Resurrection. Currently, he is completing his doctoral work in intercultural studies at Trinity International University.

Rick seeks to bring together his passions for postmodern evangelism, healing prayer and racial reconciliation to equip the emerging generation of leaders to engage and reach the contemporary world, in the United States and around the globe. He has expressed his passions in his books *Evangelism Outside the Box, Experiencing Healing Prayer* and *The Heart of Racial Justice,* coauthored with his friend Brenda Salter McNeil.

If you are interested in having Rick speak or consult, or you are interested in pursuing masters-level studies in evangelism, leadership and culture, you can contact Rick at Rick.C.Richardson@wheaton.edu.

REIMAGINING EVANGELISM CURRICULUM

An interactive multimedia curriculum based on *Reimagining Evangelism* will be released by InterVarsity Press during autumn 2007. In addition to the book, the Reimagining Evangelism Curriculum will include the *Reimagining Evangelism* DVD (6 sessions, including a Leader's Guide), and a corresponding *Reimagining Evangelism Participant's Guide*. (Each can be ordered separately.)

This easy to use curriculum, with stimulating discussions starters, thought-provoking interviews and informative teaching, will include session topics such as

- being travel guides rather than traveling sales people
- collaborating with the Holy Spirit instead of doing it all on our own
- building *genuine* friendships and starting *natural* spiritual conversations
- going beyond the testimony "script" to tell real life-change stories
- telling the *big story* of God's way of transforming people and the world
- inviting people make a commitment to God

REIMAGINING RESOURCES

If you are interested in exploring how seeker small groups, also called "groups investigating God," could be used by you or your church to reach your friends, consider the following resources.

The Groups Investigating God series is designed to be a safe place to explore your ideas about God. It is great for discussions with two or more people. There are also personal stories to read and questions to explore through journaling. Whatever you believe, there is room for you here.

> *Be prepared for the possibility that you may*
> *never look at faith the same way again.*
>
> LEE STROBEL,
> AUTHOR OF *THE CASE FOR CHRIST*

If you want some great resources for talking about Jesus in outside-the-box ways, you couldn't do better than the two below.

Don Everts speaks about Jesus in fresh and powerful ways. Seekers and believers will be changed by these books!

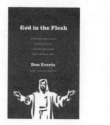

And here are a number of resources that can help you and your ministry speak about Jesus well and winsomely. *Kingdom Come* will help you understand more deeply the gospel of the kingdom of God. *Growing Your Faith by Giving It Away* is filled with stories and inspiration to grow your faith by sharing it with others. If you feel called to proclaim the good news, *Going Public with the Gospel* is especially for you.

Finally, here are some other reimagining resources from Rick Richardson. *Evangelism Outside the Box* will equip your church with new ways of helping people experience the good news. *Experiencing Healing Prayer* will teach and train you and your church to receive and minister healing to the brokenhearted. And *The Heart of Racial Justice* will lead you and your church into racial and ethnic reconciliation and healing.

A man comes across an ancient enemy, beaten and left for dead. He lifts the wounded man onto the back of a donkey and takes him to an inn to tend to the man's recovery. Jesus tells this story and instructs those who are listening to "go and do likewise."

Likewise books explore a compassionate, active faith lived out in real time. When we're skeptical about the status quo, Likewise books challenge us to create culture responsibly. When we're confused about who we are and what we're supposed to be doing, Likewise books help us listen for God's voice. When we're discouraged by the troubled world we've inherited, Likewise books encourage us to hold onto hope.

In this life we will face challenges that demand our response. Likewise books face those challenges with us so we can act on faith.

LIKEWISE.　　*Go and do.*